ETHICS INCORPORATED

Praise for the first edition

*Gupta not only clarifies what ethics means when applied
to business but also offers a step-by-step
roadmap to its implementation.*
—Business Today

Ethics Incorporated is a timely and well plotted book.
—Business Standard

*Gupta prescribes properly codified ethical practices...
(H)e goes into the specifics of what is and
what is not business ethics....*
—Hindustan Times

*Ethics Incorporated, a pioneering effort by Gupta...
is a good guide for any CEO who would like to
implement concepts of business ethics in a
practical manner in his organisation.*
—India Today

*Dr Dipankar Gupta has done a commendable job in
discussing issues like corporate governance, corporate
social responsibility, and even the link between business
ethics and social reform.... Surely, books like this
will help raise the standards of Indian business and
bring business ethics to the forefront.*
**—N.R. Narayana Murthy, Chairman and Chief
Mentor, Infosys,** *at the launch of the first edition*

ETHICS INCORPORATED

Top Priority and Bottom Line

Revised Edition

Dipankar Gupta

Response Books
A division of Sage Publications
New Delhi ♦ Thousand Oaks ♦ London

First published in 2004 by Harper Collins Publishers India

This revised edition published in 2006 by

Response Books
A division of Sage Publications
B-42, Panchsheel Enclave
New Delhi 110 017

Sage Publications Inc   **Sage Publications Ltd**
2455 Teller Road   1 Oliver's Yard, 55 City Road
Thousand Oaks, California 91320   London EC1Y 1SP

Second Printing 2006

Published by Tejeshwar Singh for Response Books, phototypeset in 10.5/13 Palatino Linotype by Star Compugraphics Private Limited, Delhi and printed at Chaman Enterprises, New Delhi.

Library of Congress Cataloging-in-Publication Data

Gupta, Dipankar, 1949–
    Ethics incorporated: top priority and bottom line/Dipankar Gupta.—
Rev. ed.
        p. cm.
    Includes bibliographical references and index.
    1. Business ethics. I. Title.

HF5387.G87   174'.4—dc22   2006   2006015494

ISBN: 10: 0–7619–3470–7 (HB)   10: 81–7829–686–1 (India HB)
       13: 978–0–7619–3470–7 (HB)   13: 978–81–7829–686–9 (India HB)
       10: 0–7619–3471–5 (PB)   10: 81–7829–685–3 (India PB)
       13: 978–0–7619–3471–4 (PB)   13: 978–81–7829–685–2 (India PB)

Production Team: R.A.M. Brown and Santosh Rawat

CONTENTS

PREFACE TO THE REVISED EDITION

Working for over six years with KPMG's Business Ethics and Integrity division in Delhi has convinced me that the Indian corporate structure is not as negative about ethical business as it is often made out to be. KPMG started this service in India with just two of us in 1999 — my namesake Deepankar Sanwalka and I. Deepankar Sanwalka not only spells his name differently from the way I do, but his core specialization is also very different from mine. While I have spent several years in the university system teaching social sciences, Deepankar Sanwalka is a chartered accountant and a certified fraud examiner as well. I like to think that this combination is just right, and the fact that our division has grown over the years makes me believe that there are many others who have the same impression as well.

I had always hoped to find a way to study corporate cultures from within and indeed contribute towards its understanding and self-awareness. Through this book I have tried to project the importance of normative interventions in corporate culture and to do that it is necessary to appreciate its inner logic, even *telos*. Fortunately I had a lot of help from other members of my team who are very bright and dynamic young people with qualifications ranging from chartered accountancy to business management to social sciences. We bring this diverse mix of specialization to bear upon any job and convert every assignment into a knowledge-producing mission.

I must confess that when we began our assignments we did not have a clearly formulated idea of how to put business ethics to work other than a set of guidelines in which we firmly believed. We were convinced that if business ethics was to make any advance then it must be able to articulate itself in practice and show empirically verifiable deliverables. To that extent we had to clarify what we meant by ethics, and why ethics is not just about being good and moral. For us, ethics is a very 'this-worldly' affair and it is not a subset of morality. Ethics demands the buy-in of 'other people' and it is not something one can practice in solitude. Ethics must be demonstrable in its effects and it does this by a transparent operationalization of norms into policies for all to see. In ethics there are no hidden agendas.

Obviously dialogy is an important element of ethical practice. Without communication, empathy and intersubjectivity, one cannot even begin to think ethically. In our case too, our commitment to the principles of dialogy and intersubjectivity helped to guide us in our many assignments on business ethics. With these lodestars we have endeavoured to add value to executive interventions that are inspired by ethical considerations. The challenge really is to present business ethics in a clearly workable fashion such that it can be readily put to use in a specific working environment. True, there is the need to constantly practice and finesse ethical programmes and systems, but higher levels of efficacy can be achieved not by pious statements but by putting forward realizable deliverables whose value can be immediately appreciated.

We learnt a lot about Business Ethics on the job, and this book is a way of expressing our gratitude to all those who had trust and faith in us in the early years. We still do not believe in off-the-shelf policy recommendations, but we do have a clearer set of guidelines and a more determined and experienced team to carry out specific projects. While we do not have readymade policy direct-ives, and we do not believe in them, yet our framework is permanently characterized by the attributes of em-pathy, dialogy and intersubjecitvity. This helps us customize our product and yet retain our stamp and our distinctive qualities. In the ultimate analysis, ex-ecutive interventions can be ethical only when these markers are self-consciously highlighted.

Though this book is being published in India, it is not an India book. The problems mentioned here, and the strategies discussed, are international in their scope. Executives everywhere would like an operational and unambiguous ethical system in their organizations. They would like to function in an atmosphere that brings out the best in them and in their team. That is why they turn to Business Ethics, and it would be a shame if at that point business ethics advocates let the side down by offering obtuse and moralistic advice.

On a personal note I must thank all the members of KPMG's Business Ethics Division. Without them this book would have been impossible. So many of the ideas and issues discussed in the following pages have emerged from actual practice in which all of us have been so deeply involved over the past several years. But to begin at the beginning, none of this would have hap-pened but for Rupendra Singh's foresight and acumen. There was no precedent of such a specialization in the developing world, and there was no reason to trust any of us as we had no proven skills in this direction. Yet he held firm in his resolve and provided us with the cover we needed to grow and establish ourselves. Jim Hunter's long distance encouragement to our work here in India helped shore up our confidence. On several occasions he found the time to come over all the way from Toronto to participate in, and help us with, what we were striving to do in our neck of the woods.

Undoubtedly, the compulsion to get real and make a difference made us more nuanced in our approach to Business Ethics. We realized the importance of cleaning up one's own backyard before going outside the factory gates as well as the significance of professionalizing the small supplier in rural India through social auditing.

I must acknowledge the unstinting and unconditional support I received from Gaganpreet Singh Puri and Kenneth Khalkho. They went through the draft closely and pointed several errors and omissions. It is indeed very difficult to read and edit somebody else's work and I am, therefore, deeply indebted to them. There are others in KPMG that have also contributed towards the making of this book but they are too numerous to name. Nevertheless, I am very grateful to them for being ever obliging and considerate.

It is a cliché to say that one lives and learns, but this adage certainly applies in the field of Business Ethics. This is because the ethical standards keep getting higher and it is important to keep abreast of these developments if one is to survive in this competitive world. We are, therefore, also grateful to those who gave us a chance to work with them.

Dipankar Gupta

CHAPTER ONE

GETTING IT RIGHT

What Is Business Ethics and What It Is Not

Ethics as a Concern for 'Others'

Before we begin to discuss Business Ethics let us first ask the question: 'What is Ethics?'

Ethics is when social interactions are premised on the unquestioned belief that the self and other deserve equal consideration. It is not at all necessary to know who these other people are or where they come from. They can be nameless and faceless and yet in a very fundamental sense their lives, hopes and ambitions are intertwined with our own, and cannot be realized separately.

Therefore, when we are talking about Ethics there is an unqualified assumption that there be, first and foremost, a quality of sameness that must be accepted universally by all social interlocutors. Once this is admitted only then is it possible to realize differences, and even encourage them in collectively approved ways.

This reminds me of what T.H. Marshall (1977) had to say about citizenship. In a much quoted work Marshall argued that citizenship insists on the equality of individuals as citizens. Once this is ensured then people can develop unequally and in different directions. What may seem good for one may not appear attractive to another. Moreover different individuals may have different levels of aspirations, talents and grit, and all of these will lead to inequalities in the end. But in none of these instances can it be said that there is stark inequality at the starting point between citizens. It is not surprising, therefore, that ethics and citizenship should be such modern concerns.

The term 'other people' needs clarification for it can lead to conclusions that are far from ethical. For example if we are only concerned in our social interactions with certain named and specific people then that would not be ethical, but would verge instead towards favouritism, clientelism, and worse. When other people are seen in named and specific ways, and not in universal terms, then the adage 'do unto others as you would have them do unto you' could also easily degenerate into a species of 'you scratch my back and I will scratch yours'.

In pre-modern times it was not ethics that dominated our thinking, but morality. Morality was about the self, and about attaining high levels of spiritual or other kinds of perfection. In the final analysis it did not really matter what others did or said so long as the self could pursue a personalized moral goal, if necessarily all on one's own. We will return to this subject a little later.

Ethics, on the other hand, is not an individual attribute as it is a quality that marks social interactions. In other words, one cannot be ethical alone as it becomes relevant only in the context of social relations. But only those interactions are ethical which are premised on a concern for 'other people'. Ethics seek justification in the lives of mortals and not in the eyes of God. This also implies that people have a definite stake in upholding these ethical norms as there is something that is experientially valuable in them for everybody.

A quick, even trivial, example of ethics is traffic rules. In order to get to a destination in the shortest time for everybody it is best that all drive in their own lane and obey street signals. Deviations from this may work for some for some time but is collectively counter-productive.

So What Is Business Ethics?

Now that we know what ethics is let us ask the next question: 'What is Business Ethics?' Business Ethics is quite simply applying the basic principles of ethics in the realm of business-where profit is the key consideration. Let us not fudge the truth—no profit, bad business.

It is pointless to boast about being ethical if the company's balance sheet makes for dismal reading. If the employees of an organization cannot be protected, if the shareholders' trust cannot be rewarded, then there is something very wrong in the way the company is being run.

To say that we are losing out because we are ethical is a very lame excuse. Business Ethics is not about withdrawal from activism. It must be understood instead as a hardy and practical guide, which when properly put in place, helps top management to negotiate corporate activity in a complex and competitive world.

Business Ethics demands that profit be made on a sustainable basis by observing norms that respect other people. Fairness, transparency, and individual ambitions must all find a place in the practice of Business Ethics. What needs to be continuously emphasized is that individual goals cannot be attained separately and that there is a common horizon within which everybody functions. The success of a company depends on its ability to create a culture which makes clear to the naked eye that individual gain is an integral part of collective profit. This demands that all functionaries in a corporate unit pull together as a team.

The mention of the word 'team' may appear like another trivial metaphor, but consider the following: In a sport it is the job of the captain to draw out the best from the team and for the referee to unambiguously draw the line regarding what cannot be done by anybody—not even the captain. These rules are laid out in advance and not applied capriciously. Only then is it possible to think of winners and losers, and only then is it also possible to bring out the best in the players.

It is true that there are short cuts to making money, and it is also true that there are many unethical business magnates who even break the law and get away with it. This often gives the impression that if a company were to adopt an ethical system it would be seriously handicapped. No doubt, there are many who are persuaded by this argument but that is because they view ethics as a restrictive set of injunctions and not as an enabling tool.

Quick profits, unfair employment policies, tampering with the integrity of records might bring short term benefits but do not generate pride in workmanship or partnership and respect among co-workers and stakeholders. Short cuts make selective friends for they privilege named and specific others, while ethics, which is for the marathon runner, creates long term capacities among stakeholders in general. In the ultimate analysis for an enterprise to succeed it needs its stakeholders to back it all the way. Selective others are always tricky customers and, at best, fair weather friends.

Business Ethics is not just obeying the law but raising standards.

Neither is Business Ethics synonymous with legality. Doing things legally is a necessary but not sufficient condition for Business Ethics. If one is all too eager to break the law and make a quick profit then obviously ethics is of no concern whatsoever to that person. But obeying the law does not necessarily imply that there is a willing concern for norms that create a feeling of togetherness, of pulling together as a team, or of realizing individual ambitions collectively.

One can observe the law and yet be unmindful of fair hiring policies: likewise it is clearly possible to go by the book on wages and benefits without paying attention to employee grievances or for upskilling them. Similarly, pollution laws can be adhered to but doubtful chemicals that have not yet been legally banned could still be a product ingredient. On many occasions it has been observed that contract labour stipulations are scrupulously followed by companies but care is taken not to exceed the minimum number of workers stipulated by law under each contractor in order to escape trade union rules. Such examples can be multiplied and every executive is aware of these manoeuvres.

Let us then end the preliminaries by posing clear alternatives. If it is in your disposition to get rich through sharp practices then obviously Business Ethics is not for you. On the other hand, if entrepreneurs are looking at the big picture and want to remain effective players over the long run by carrying their stakeholders with them, then it would be wise to pay attention to the principles of Business Ethics wherein a commitment to 'others' is essential for the realizing of personal goals.

Thinking in terms of Business Ethics is really thinking *leadership*. Do we want to run a business that lacks cohesion and direction, and where surveillance replaces initiatives? Do we want to manage a firm where the leader can establish dominance through fear, or by precept? The content and context of corporate leadership has changed immensely in modern times. Leadership in business today requires skills that were not recognized as such in the past. Business leaders are team leaders who recognize that talent is not located just at the top. According to *Fortune* magazine, the top fifteen American companies also figure amongst the twenty most loved companies in the country. So somewhere it pays to be ethical, but how does one go about it?

In the case of Business Ethics it is imperative that the programme be *top driven*. The seniormost executives must be committed to Business Ethics and should be willing to lead by example if they are serious about making a difference in their establishments. In my experience, the appreciation of Business Ethics does not depend on the type of industry, but really on the commitment at the top. Looked at this way, Business Ethics is really an arena where leadership is paramount.

It is imperative for Business Ethics to be top driven.

The problem, however, is that nobody is really sure what is meant by Business Ethics. It becomes difficult for many senior managers to adopt the Business Ethics process in the face of pre-existing cynicism regarding it. Does Business Ethics mean that we become otherworldly and forsake material prosperity? In that case, why be in business at all?

Does it mean to obey the law? So what is new about that? Does it mean to spread your profits around by doing social work and philanthropy? In that case, how does all that really connect with business?

This is why I believe that it is of primary importance to rid the concept of Business Ethics of its various misconceptions. There is a clear and persistent demand from the information technology (IT) sector, multinational fast moving consumer goods organizations and diversified Indian players to clarify what is meant by Business Ethics, and to demonstrate its practical necessity. The top executives tend to value its importance once there is clarity on the subject. It is sometimes argued that IT enterprises are more favourably disposed towards Business Ethics than other companies, but this argument cannot be consistently sustained. A lot depends on the leadership of the company and not so much on the kind of goods and services that enterprises specialize in.

Therefore, to begin with, it is worthwhile to make clear what Business Ethics is and what it is not.

1. *Business Ethics*

Is not about morality, but about the establishment of transparent norms of interrelationships.

Morality can be an individual set of commitments and a person can live with them even when they are rejected by others. But one cannot be ethical alone. Ethics brings in 'other people' for the realization of the self.

2. *Business Ethics*

Is socially aware entrepreneurship and *not just* philanthropy. An ethical business enterprise demonstrates its social concern through its internal functioning and is not limited to acts of philanthropy. When an organization's involvement in wider social affairs stems from concerns within, its activism outside is more consistent and capable of systemic expansion.

ETHICS INCORPORATED

3. Business Ethics

Is respectful of the stakeholder and *not just* the shareholder.

The stakeholder includes not just the shareholder, but also employees, customers, creditors as well as dealers.

4. Business Ethics

Is concerned with a code of ethics and *not just* with a code of conduct.

When the code of conduct flows from the code of ethics it gets internalized as a normative value. It no longer remains an external instrument of control.

5. Business Ethics

Is about establishing employee morale and *not just* about establishing compliance.

Employee morale depends a great deal on commitment to the specific culture of the organization, and not just to formal agreements and negotiations.

6. Business Ethics

Is committed to quality arising out of work satisfaction and *not just* for reasons of profit.

Quality production is best ensured by making sure that employees are intellectually contributing to the work process and not just following orders. This helps to sustain profits more enduringly than advertising, cost cutting, or pure technological inputs.

These issues are elaborated further in the following pages.

Beginning at Home

As clarified, Business Ethics is neither about philanthropy nor about occupying high moral ground. In fact, the best ethics begins at the beginning: at the workplace, and with the people one works with.

The best ethics begins at the beginning: at the workplace, and with people one works with.

The two most critical features of ethical business are (i) to *know* one's company/organization, and (ii) to frame explicit rules that apply to all. So any top executive who seriously believes in these two precepts has already taken the big step towards running an ethical business.

Executives in high-performance organizations will immediately appreciate the significance of knowing one's company. A sincere and thorough accomplishment of this task is actually an illustration of Business Ethics at work. Knowing how employees in the company think, and how they react to particular situations in the context of stated rules, is absolutely essential if the organization is to fortify itself internally for facing competitors in the marketplace.

Second, all ambitious and goal-oriented top executives would like to see their vision realized in the enterprises they manage. It is, therefore, desirable for them to synergize their vision down the line with foundational norms, rules of procedure, and codes of conduct. Thinking along these lines is once again thinking ethically. So ethics is inescapable on two of the most elementary aspects of business management.

What needs to be recognized, above all else, is that the regime of Business Ethics begins in one's own backyard. All too often practitioners and advocates of Business Ethics are dragging senior executives to sites far away from the workplace, to villages, schools, hospitals, etc. Or they are asked to subscribe to values that are very progressive, from gender equality to good environment, without linking them directly to the nature of their job and expertise. Worthy though these efforts are, by themselves they leave senior executives indifferent and disinterested.

Know Your Company

Knowing your company is the first step in Business Ethics. All chief executive officers and members of the top management would like to know their company. If you think you know your company then ask yourself whether you got this knowledge from:

    (a) talking to your trusted colleagues;
    (b) the kinds of grievances raised over the years;
    (c) the way in which people react to different issues at meetings; and
    (d) your own experiences in trying to get things done.

Doubtless, each one of us, in our own way, has a feel of the organization for which we work. But as a leader of the firm, this knowledge needs to be structured and open to objective assessment. All too often the information is incomplete and perhaps not critically evaluated. Equally important, if not more, is to know how other people, your colleagues and subordinates, think of the organization for which they work. To get a measure of this, it is necessary to garner information through workshops across levels and functions within the enterprise. Have you done that?

If you know your organization inside out then you will have a focused understanding on a variety of important and critical areas:

(a) You will know what others in the organization think of your mission and vision programmes. This should help you strategize and operationalize your goals more effectively.

(b) You will also know what kinds of information blocks exist within the organization. This might happen despite the fact that great care has been taken to be open and accessible to subordinates.

(c) You will be aware of the multiple ways in which the most elementary rules and management values are interpreted. This will help clarify misperceptions.

These are just some of the immediate advantages of knowing your company by soliciting information across the board and through workshops that are conducted in a dialogical fashion. Dialogical, in this sense, only means the willingness to hear and appreciate other points of view within a structured setting. Taking this first step in Business Ethics demonstrates the willingness of the top executives to examine, refine, and if necessary, *When top executives dare to know, they no longer shy away from unpleasant truths.*

modify rules, regulations and even vision and mission statements of the company, in an interactive setting. Other employees, staff and workers in the company are viewed as stakeholders, rather than merely as subordinates.

Knowing your company is not a gesture in goodwill, but is driven by practical business interests. Company policies need to be realistic and forward looking without being wordy (for that results in cynicism). Finally, they should be effective. Which chief executive officer would not like any of these?

However, not everybody has the stomach to really know the company, because not everybody is driven by a sense of being truly ethical. But when top executives 'Dare to Know' (see Kant 1983: 47), they are putting in practice an 'enlightenment' ideal to their ethical commitment where it counts most—at the workplace. When they dare to know, they no longer shy away from unpleasant truths.

CSR and Modernity

This change in attitude towards co-workers and employees is because the levels of technology are now so advanced that no single person, or department, can corner it and hope to control it for the company as a whole. With the social spread of technology at every level of expertise there has to be a greater respect down the line if the firm is to function as a cohesive unit. Second, in keeping with the changes in technology there has been a general elevation of expectations regarding standards on the part of consumers of goods and services. Both of these features can be tracked down to the overall development of partnership in an organization where individual merit and needs are recognized as intrinsically worthy of promotion.

These tectonic changes in modern societies have flattened status considerations that were so much a part of the pre-modern era. The 'other' now begins to figure in the way one individuates oneself. This has become a structural condition of modern societies and it has nothing to do with altruism or generosity. While this trait is developed quite prominently in most western societies, it is also making headway in countries like India, though there is still a long distance to travel. But that is the general direction and it is, therefore, advisable to recognize it and put our corporate practices in line with it. This is why it is imperative now to think in terms of Business Ethics where considerations of the 'other' are crucial for any entrepreneurial venture that hopes to last the distance over the long haul.

From Implicit to Explicit

There will always be some kind of norm, or cluster of norms, in the functioning of any business house. There can be no organization of personnel, indeed, no interaction among human beings, which is not presumed on some norm or the other.

However, in the absence of an explicit set of rules, implicit rules gradually evolve. This gives the management a choice. Do they want formulation of explicit rules or let implicit ones emerge with the passage of time, and through experience. Implicit rules have an allure about them for they are already in practice and seem eminently workable. They are like good old shoes, but are they sensible as well?

Implicit rules tend to be open ended, equivocal, capable of diverse interpretations, and, in reality, much more authoritarian in their disposition than what might appear at first glance. Implicit rules generally reflect existing power equations. They also give credibility to the 'line of least resistance' policy. Consequently, there is a willingness to compromise on practically everything, as long as the short-term objectives are met.

Any ambitious and imaginative management leader will immediately recognize the inherent dangers of such implicit rules. Their most egregious drawback is that *Implicit rules are* they are open to multiple and contra- *dangerous as they* dictory interpretations of basic values *are open to multiple* and policies of the company. These con- *interpretations.* tradictions create the greatest obstacle to clear and transparent communication.

Thus when implicit ethics is unsupported by explicit ethics, it is difficult to ensure transparency and accountability. 'Show me the person and I will tell you the rule,' will become the order of the day.

As ethics is really about how we relate to other people, it is impossible to escape it, one way or another. Given this reality, is it not better to be clear about what the organization stands for? This is why it pays to formulate, as explicitly as possible, the company's foundational values and code of business conduct.

Once ethical policies are formally in place they need to be continually supported by implicit ethics. If explicit ethics says, 'This is who we are,' then implicit ethics should back it up by demonstrating, 'This is how we do things around here.' It is clearly not enough to have an explicit ethical policy that is not operationalized in terms of everyday, routine activities.

The tone and working of managers and supervisors must be in line with the explicitly formulated ethical documents. Official policy and regulations lose force when everyone knows that certain questionable market practices are either condoned or unofficially encouraged. The written pledge to do the right thing should not be subverted in practice by doing whatever it takes to achieve performance targets.

When there is a conflict between explicit and implicit elements of the ethics process, then implicit ethics will prevail. To prevent this from happening it is necessary to achieve a high degree of concordance between these two ethical realms.

Explicit	Implicit
Written documents	Culture of the organization
Training sessions	Management example
Chief executive officer speeches	Valued behaviours
Reward and sanctions structure	Actual performance measures

Implicit ethics runs between the lines of explicit ethics. Unless the two are mutually supportive, written ethical documents are likely to be cast aside. Employees would find it both easier and more practical to read between the lines and ignore the bold print.

It is best then to set out explicit rules of an organization. In order to make this set of explicit rules, an ethical business leader would like to test the views and ambitions of the boardroom against reactions from the lower levels. Not only does this make company regulations and rules, from the vision statement to the code of conduct and general office procedures, more workable, but ensures uniform understanding of these. People now know what to expect from others with much greater clarity. Without explicit rules, *it is difficult to know your company.*

Before these explicit rules are actually put to work they should be ethically whetted through dialogical workshops. At the end, the organization should have a clear, unambiguous written policy on ethics, on business procedures and on norms of collegiate interactions. This must have the buy-in of the widest section of the employees. The *end result* of an ethical process is a written document. All too often, top management *begins* with a written document and then wonders what went wrong, where and why.

The moment senior management realizes the importance of 'knowing your company' and putting in place 'explicit rules', the process of Business Ethics is well under way. To be ethical there is no need for any talk of morality, or of philanthropy, or of digging wells, or of providing drinking water to distant villages. Morality and philanthropy are, in that sense, optional. We will return to these points later. But for now the emphasis is that to put in practice the principles of Business Ethics one has to begin literally from one's desk, right there in the place of work, keeping uppermost in mind issues that concern business. After all, the purpose of the organization, the fundamental reason for its being, must always be uppermost (Hartman 1998: 125).

Looked at this way, Business Ethics begins its career in your enterprise as a practical and useful tool that helps in raising levels of communication and efficiency among all categories of employees. This is another form of adding value. Indeed, this can also be measured. Ethical benchmarks can be drawn to aid a comparative assessment of the levels of unanimity in the understanding of company policies and the extent of buy-in on matters beginning from the vision statement to office procedures.

Ethical reviews, benchmarking and workshops can give you answers to the following questions: Are some of the rules outdated/irrelevant? Do they need to be revised? And very importantly, are the officials, staff, employees, managers, and executives, able to handle ethical dilemmas adroitly?

So if you are a chief executive officer, or someone who aspires to be a chief executive officer one day, and you do not want to 'know your company', or you do not believe in setting up 'explicit rules' that are transparent in origin and intent, then this book is not for you.

Ethics and Philanthropy

In an influential essay entitled 'Social Responsibility of Business', Nobel laureate Milton Friedman argued that the espousal of 'social responsibilities' by the corporate sector was not just bad for business, but was tantamount to a frank and outright advocacy of unadulterated socialism. Friedman's essay was first published in 1970 in *The New York Times Magazine*, but it should combatively engage scholars and activists even today. Friedman's argument briefly was that a corporate executive's responsibility stopped with the shareholder and went no further. As long as executives make sure that they are functioning within the law, their prime concern should be to promote and protect the interests of those who have invested in the company. Anything beyond that is a betrayal of trust and rank bad judgment. Friedman, however, conceded that corporate executives, as individuals, could donate some of their earnings and time to charitable causes (see Friedman 1987: 39). But this should not, on any account, be merged with their responsibilities as managers of shareholders' investment, funds and trust.

I agree with Professor Friedman that a corporate executive's job description does not include haring around from cause to cause trying to be a petty mahatma. It is also true that media-enriched charity events often deflect attention from the job of running efficient and rule-abiding enterprises. But Friedman's understanding of corporate social responsibility was very narrow as he restricted its meaning to philanthropy and little else. With the arrival of Business Ethics as an articulated corporate practice, the conception of corporate social responsibility has gone well beyond the donor mentality. Business Ethics successfully merges social responsibility with the imperatives of corporate efficiency in a fashion that is hard-nosed, pragmatic, and bottom line-oriented. We now know that it is not enough for business people to stay within the law and make their money—recent studies have shown that businesses are rewarded when they are ethical as well. What is more, ethical business practices meet social responsibilities much more wholesomely than corporate philanthropy can ever hope to do.

The conception of corporate social responsibility has gone well beyond the donor mentality.

A company's external image as a social do-gooder is not germane to Business Ethics. It is only when an organization's external profile is an outgrowth of its ethical practices within that Milton Friedman's objections can be truly met. An ethical practice does not privilege profit at any cost, but sets up norms of functioning that are *transparent* in every respect. It is this transparency that *adds* to the bottom line on a more enduring basis. Customers know exactly what they are getting, the employees are assured that nobody is playing favourites within the organization, and the shareholders are satisfied that the company is keeping them fully informed about its activities. Faulting on any one of these minimal characteristics of Business Ethics would immediately violate the transparency requirement. Therefore, it is not enough to just operate within the law, it is important to be ethical as well.

In fact much of the social devastation we see around us is because organizations, both public and private, do not work ethically. Ethical practice is under great strain in an unethical environment. In such conditions it is easier to be moral than ethical. Morality is a virtue that lends itself easily to privatization. Indeed the more unethical the environment the greater the tendency, and scope, for individuals to grandstand as philanthropists. (As Hegel once observed, 'men would rather be magnanimous than law abiding'.) While philanthropy is to be recommended, it cannot take the place of Business Ethics. It is necessary to recognize, though it may sometimes be distressing, that a philanthropic organization can often be unethical in terms of how it handles its immediate stakeholders.

This is what makes it imperative to link ethics with principles of functioning that can be immediately operationalized and reproduced across the board. An organization's philanthropic character can now be measured on another scale. An ethical enterprise is not concerned so much about being a do-good organization, but its very internal functioning radiates outward to create a positive impact on social concerns.

Why Ethics and Morality Are Not Synonyms

As will be evident from the discussion so far, ethics is not about pulpit preaching, nor about religious hectoring. In fact, ethics, in the true sense of the term, has nothing to do with either of these. Neither does the imperative of knowing your company, or setting up explicit ethical norms for organizational functioning, imply soaring above the clouds. In plain terms, *ethics is a very practical approach towards attaining goals in an environment that involves other people.*

In the words of Emanuel Levinas, ethics is an awareness of *other people*, such that a person is 'individuated' by responsibility for the other. Powerful words! For Levinas then, the other is both an object of understanding and an interlocutor (Levinas 1998: 6, 86–71, 109). Ethics comes into its own when we recognize that in the pursuit of individual excellence there are other people who have to be treated with respect. Nowhere does this imply that ethics demands either boundless love or self-sacrifice. Ethics is really a temperate and tepid disposition (Krygier 1997). It merely insists that 'other people' are significant variables that need to be factored in when we devise strategies to pursue our goals.

If we keep this in mind then we can bring Business Ethics to the shop floor and not remain 35,000 feet above sea level. If ethics is about other people then can any modern corporate organization really afford to ignore ethical imperatives behind business management?

Morality, unlike ethics, can be privatized, and indeed, it often is. Morality does not demand acquiescence from others the way ethics does. In other words, it is possible to be moral alone. In fact, many times a moralist gets a charge by being in a sea of immoral people. This is how the moralist stands out. A moralist might say that I do not believe in war, so what if everybody else does? A moralist might be a vegetarian amongst carnivores, or an advocate of plain living while others take recourse to gadgets of all description. As the moralist is not pressured to make morals workable or acceptable to others, such a person could quite easily stay alone, or on the margins of society. Such a person may also draw secondary gratification from this loneliness that would seem to validate the core of his moral commitment. It is, of course, widely known that moralists can sometimes have a strong effect on others in society, but this is not because of any active act of volition on the part of the moralist.

Morality can be privatized but not ethics, which is about other people.

As morals are not forced to be generally effective and win wide acceptance, certain ethical norms may often conflict with moral values (see Berlin 1981: 50–64). For example, the morality in being a good and caring parent can run against the sanctions on nepotism. Morality may also compel one to abide by norms of purity and pollution, or by racial and religious considerations, but such practices invariably cause hierarchies and separate other members of society in a permanently unequal way. The prejudices that such kinds of morality let loose are not open for close scrutiny, as it is something that a person believes in for its own sake and not because it has any proven track record. As Levinas helped us understand, ethics would find this unacceptable for the 'others' are not equal and active interlocutors with the self.

Morals can be adhered to because they are considered good in themselves and not because of their proven ability to achieve desired collective goals. Even if others do not participate in a particular moral persuasion, a person's moral standards can remain unchanged. For example, filial piety or vegetarianism is often a moral imperative. This does not, however, imply that those who subscribe to these values do so because they want to be remembered in their ancestor's will, or, in the latter case, because they want to live longer. Unlike ethics, morals are thus not pressured to objectively demonstrate the efficacy of morality, and this is what really separates the two. Ethics must always, without exception, translate its norms into policies that have demonstrable positive effects. This is why ethics is so important in the making of organizational norms.

Business Ethics and Organizational Norms

The reason why explicit norms matter is because they encourage contributions from internal stakeholders, such as colleagues, staff and workers, thus making a positive difference to organizational health. Who would want a chaotic office where there are a myriad rules which can mean any number of things (Kaptein 1998)?

It is only when rules are properly established that people are truly challenged and perform at their best.

But what most cynical executives do not realize is that the moment they opt for a well-laid-out system of norms to govern interactions at work they are actually calling out to Business Ethics. In this sense, Business Ethics, as we mentioned earlier, is actually inescapable. The launching of such a system of working rules and norms can be done best only if one proceeds along the ground rules laid by ethics. This simply means that one must think of 'others' in the workplace and, by extension, of those whose lives are impinged by one's work, even as one pursues one's goal. In fact, one can go further and claim that it is only when rules are properly established in an unambiguous fashion, that people are truly challenged and perform at their best. Such, at least, is the burden of Norbert Elias's splendid work entitled *Civilizing Process* (Elias 1978).

The insistence that these ethical norms be established dialogically also brings in the significance of the 'other'. It is important that there be a genuine endorsement of the stated business principles, codes of conduct, mission and vision statements across divisions and levels in the organization. In this way ethics teaches us how to move from pure power to genuine authority.

Even when there is a recognition that rules have to be laid out, there is a tendency to pronounce them from above—tycoon style. Where societies are marked by deep fissures of class and status it is all the more difficult to recognize the 'other' (recall Levinas), as one's consistent interlocutor. But times have changed since the early robber baron days. The presence of the other, which in this case means the stakeholder, is all too pressing to be overlooked.

The 'other' comes in on a variety of fronts. Not only is the 'other' a substantive equal who demands and receives respect, but the 'other', in any vital business firm, is also one who contributes essentially towards the development of the organization's well-being. As the 'other' counts, it is important that ethical norms be made demonstrable for others to judge their efficacy and worth.

And, as we said earlier, the 'others' begin right there in the place of work. There is nothing like cleaning up one's own backyard before stepping out to take on the world. Indeed, if the procedures and principles are ethically mandated 'at home', that is, within the factory gates, it gives executives the strength and the confidence to pursue market goals more aggressively.

The Significance of the Stakeholder Perspective

It is now widely recognized that stakeholders add to a company's well-being in a variety of ways. The shareholders by putting in money, employees by contributing their expertise on the job, customers by buying products and services that an enterprise has to offer, and members of the community by supporting the organization as a corporate citizen. In other words, a stakeholder is anyone who has a 'legitimate interest' in the firm (see Donaldson and Preston 1995: 65–91).

Obviously, each of the stakeholders expects value in return. To be able to give the stakeholders what they want also adds value to the company. But the stakeholders do not all view value in the same way. Shareholders primarily value how competitive the company is in the marketplace, and how much they can expect in terms of financial returns. Employees value respect, a kind working environment, and job satisfaction, as well as just and fair remuneration. Customers want quality products at appropriate prices. And finally, the community values environmental responsibility and forward-looking business policies that encourage upward social mobility.

While the notion of what constitutes value varies widely across different stakeholders, it is the wise management that is able to harmonize this divergence to optimum advantage. To prefer one to the exclusion of the others will not benefit the company even in the medium run. Indeed, to be sensitive to what constitutes value for different categories of stakeholders is ultimately what Business Ethics is all about.

Knowing your company leads one to take a *stakeholder view of business*. To begin with, it is necessary to know the stakeholders within the organization itself. It is important to know how employees at different levels in the hierarchy view the rules and norms of the company, and what their everyday problems are all about. Second, one should not forget the creditors and dealers, who may be external to the organization at one level but are very integral to it at another. Then there are the customers. Should we not find out what they think of our produce, and do they have some unexpressed felt needs that we might try and satisfy through the goods and services that we are in the business of providing? Finally, the community and environment in which we work must also be addressed with respect and empathy. Even though the record on this is not absolutely clinching, it can, nevertheless, still be maintained that companies that have paid attention to their environment and community have never suffered on this account.

Primitive capitalism was characterized by robber barons, red in tooth and claw, bent on thuggery, looting and bludgeoning their way to the top. Trafficking in drugs, bootlegging, and blacklegging, were all par for the course. That is why it was said that one should never ask a millionaire how he made his first million. The history of early capitalism is full of gory and grisly stories that would curdle anyone's blood. They are certainly not the kind that one would recount glowingly in ·business schools to bright young people.

Contrast this with the eagerness with which successful captains of industry today expansively relate the way to their first *billion*. When Bill Gates came to India this is all that people wanted to know. Business journals beef up their sales by carrying life stories of the rich and powerful in the corporate world, from Warren Buffet of Berkshire Hathaway to N.R. Narayana Murthy of Infosys. Their lives make good reading and do not require parental guidance.

Interestingly, the most admired companies as listed by *Fortune* magazine have built their towering reputation on ethics and public awareness. These companies have the best employee relations, do not produce commodities, like tobacco, which are harmful to consumers, and have broader ideas that align them to dominant social concerns of the day.

The most admired companies today have shifted their concern from shareholders to stakeholders.

Transparency is the *leitmotif* of such organizations, for they believe that they owe it not only to shareholders but to their stakeholders as well.

The shift in concern from shareholders and the bottom line of profit to stakeholders has made for a huge difference even on pure business considerations. Successful corporate houses in the West have developed acute sensors to pick up the faintest seismic rumble among customers, and indeed, in the community at large. This is how leaders in the business field broke away from the pack and set up an entirely different set of standards. By giving the public a feeling that they matter, such companies easily outstripped the more traditional ones that focused only on shareholders' returns.

This was product differentiation with a difference. Business leaders who had a good view from their boardrooms were now eyeing the customer, the stakeholder and the community to give their companies a high profile and a healthier bottom line. This was a wholly different tactic and it was paying off. The route was a little circuitous, no doubt. Judging, however, from the dividends of the top 10 industrial giants in America, neither the customer, nor the shareholder, seems to mind the extra distance.

In fact, some chief executive officers are getting decidedly mushy. Herb Kelleher of South Western Airlines in the US is such an affectionate hugger and kisser that his company's symbol is *LUV*. As South Western Airlines ranks sixth among the top 10 in America, the shareholders are loving it all the way to the bank. GE is reported to spend about US$ 800 million a year on leadership and training. Productivity is said to rise steeply on account of employee endorsement of the organization's mission and vision. It is on the energy waves of these born-again employees that leading companies can sermonize about how to enlarge their profit margins.

As always the most essential aspect of the sermons is non-quantifiable. All the hand-pressing and back-slapping by chief executive officers makes a difference only when organizations are committed to ethical practice. It is generally recognized that bribing is the easiest of sins to commit, but it has devastating consequences. Bribery, if encouraged, creates a sub-specialty, that of the fixers, who over time begin to take precedence over those who are enterprising and innovative. Consequently the emphasis on quality production is replaced by short-term concerns with profits and not with being a long-term leader. As sure as any law of nature, this strategy eventually leads to economic decline in the not too long run. It is in enlightened self-interest then that most respectable US companies have an uncompromising stricture on bribing.

But ethics is more than steering clear of bribes. Thou shalt not bribe, and thou shalt not fudge accounts, are accompanied by a host of prescriptive 'thou shalt' policies. A company concerned about its ethical status is also one which pays greater attention to evolving a participative corporate culture. Among other things this culture consists of effective communication between different levels, rewarding employee enterprise, and protecting whistle-blowers, no matter how iffy this might be on occasions. Nearly all such companies have ombudspersons who are either hired internally, or come in as specialist consultants from outside. These enterprises realize that it is much more cost effective to prevent fraud than to clear up the mess after it has occurred. The fate of Enron is everybody's favourite example to prove this point. This is why forensic accounting and Business Ethics practices are specialities that are internationally much sought after by confident and aggressive business concerns.

The significance of Business Ethics has yet to gain credibility in many corporate houses, especially in the developing countries. In India, companies like Eicher, Tata, Infosys, Thermax and Sanmar Industries are some of the early beginners in this field. Their business styles may be admired from afar but are not yet widely emulated. Eicher's Alwar plan, which gives the workers an active stake in the business, and Narayana Murthy's model of putting ethics before profit can yet serve as beacons for the Indian corporate sector. It is heartening to note that the Confederation of Indian Industry has taken an active interest in advancing the code of corporate governance in India.

The reluctance to adopt Business Ethics as a guide to successful corporate functioning is often on account of relying too heavily on a few big customers. In such cases there is an obvious lack of entrepreneurial dynamism that can be ruinous in the not too long run. This tendency not to challenge oneself is strengthened further in situations where the market is protected from global competition. When this happens winning approval from important government functionaries assumes enormous importance and overwhelms the entrepreneurial drive. Consequently, there is a fall in standards and quality across the board. This hurts stockholders and customers the most.

The reluctance to adopt Business Ethics is often on account of relying too heavily on a few big customers.

However, things have changed quite dramatically in recent times the world over. Controlled economies of yore are slowly beginning to transform themselves. Taking the example of India again, there was a time when permitocrats and permitocracy ruled business in this country. Now with the opening of the equity market and the entry of foreign competitors, there has been a drastic change in the situation. Consumers are becoming more conscious and shareholders more demanding. It is not as if the crippling regime of the past has left no impress whatsoever, but enterprise is struggling to break free from it. This is why today many Indian businesses are recognizing the relevance of Business Ethics.

Family Values versus Business Ethics

Family values have a way of perjuring Business Ethics, and yet very few are willing to be forthright on these matters. Family values are great so long as they

Family values are great so long as they stay within the family.

stay within the family. Family is where relationships are given not chosen. In a family, sentiments of love often overrule considerations of justice. A family is where one seeks refuge from a demanding world outside. In a family loyalty is unquestioned and nobody is turned out.

Imagine what would happen if a corporate house were run on such principles. Employees would be judged by their closeness to superiors and not by performance. Wrongdoings, sometimes really serious ones, would go unpunished because of feelings of love and affection. Rules and codes of conduct would be constantly adjusted to match the moods of idiosyncratic personnel.

In a corporate world, ethics demand that the rules of the game are stated well in advance. There is a lot of room for consideration, but little scope for indulgence. To be a functioning member of an organization it is important to stay fit, and continually practice to improve one's performance. To ask for special favours is to bring family norms into the workplace. As not everybody in the firm can be a member of the same family, some will obviously feel left out and discriminated against. This will not help in generating trust within the firm. Corporate trust does not come about by being avuncular or patriarchal, but by being fair and playing by transparent rules. Family values, when taken outside the context of the family, can and do harbour patron-client ties, favouritism, and sycophancy. It is not very easy to call a spade a spade, especially when it looks harmless.

The Three Principles of Business Ethics

To sum up then, there are three abiding principles of Business Ethics:

1. Standardization

The first principle of Business Ethics is that all rules and norms flowing from it should be equally applicable to all. In other words, *standardization* is the key. Favouritism and partiality should not be allowed. Additionally, care needs to be taken that anything that might appear as favouritism be expunged or thoroughly scrutinized before it is allowed to pass. The appearance of favouritism and double standards can be as deleterious as when these actually take place. One must not only be just, but also appear to be just.

2. Workable

The second principle of Business Ethics is that rules and norms be *workable* and show tangible benefits. The effects of Business Ethics should be objectively available to all as stated policy statements. This is why 'others' are so important for a successful implementation of Business Ethics.

3. Driven from the Top

The third rule of Business Ethics is that the *top management's complete commitment* is important to the Business Ethics programme. Business Ethics is driven from the top. Only when the top management demonstrates its commitment to Business Ethics is it likely to work. Business Ethics is not only about being legal, but about being ethically correct as well.

None of these three principles can be undermined or cast aside. They make sense as a composite unity and not individually.

Luxury or Necessity

Is Business Ethics a luxury that only hugely profitable companies can afford? Is Business Ethics a frivolous and expensive indulgence of a few ego-centred chief executive officers?

Not true!

The principal aim of a Business Ethics programme is to create a distinctive culture within the organization.

Business Ethics principles, appropriately applied, have helped many struggling companies to turn their fortunes around. But one need not wait for a crisis to adopt Business Ethics. In fact Business Ethics does even better in normal times.

The principal aim of a Business Ethics programme is to create a distinctive culture within the organization of which everybody, high and low, can be justly proud. This is the most critical factor. To bring this about requires careful planning and not just a shower of goodwill.

The rise and fall of many corporate empires is not always because of bad investment decisions. Several established business houses have fallen because of a vitiated work atmosphere, the most spectacular case being that of Enron.

Think of the pure advantages of evolving a distinctive culture that is positively endorsed by managers and workers in a company. A committed cadre reduces employee turnover at all levels. This in itself is a huge saving, particularly for high-technology industries. Studies also show that there is a huge incidence of turnover and burnout among chief executive officers as well. This is both individually worrisome and collectively expensive. When a vibrant and bonding culture is absent within an enterprise only the top executive feels responsible. This puts an extraordinary quantum of pressure on chief executive officers of such organizations, as if only *they* are supposed to perform.

Business Ethics has other advantages too. Employees do not just mark time waiting for the most opportune moment to strike. Even petty expenditures (which can add up to a lot) come down, as the company is not seen as a cash cow to be milked at will. Further, discipline emerges not from the heavy hand of punitive sanctions but because workers feel responsible and committed to their job.

Living in a Fish Bowl

It is often believed that culture 'determines how people behave when they are not being watched.' However, this is an incomplete understanding of culture, and can be misleading, especially when devising appropriate Business Ethics systems for the corporate world.

To begin with culture is not what people do when they are on their own, but when they are interacting with one another. In which case, minimally, at least one person is looking. Culture makes no sense when there is only a Robinson Crusoe. Introduce a Man Friday and immediately culture kicks in.

Business Ethics demands that one should function as if one is always in full public view.

Business Ethics depends on creating a definite culture that involves and enthuses all employees within an organization. Quite naturally, Business Ethics demands that cultural norms be translatable in practice in such a manner that relations between people are transparent and unambiguous. This entails that relations with subordinates, or with superiors, or with equals, be on terms that are acceptable to everybody across the board. Act, therefore, as if everybody is looking.

This obviously implies that culture is what one does in the open. And even if not everybody is watching, imagine a hypothetical situation when you are in full view of all your colleagues (both superiors and subordinates), when you interact with any one of them.

Bronislaw Malinowski, arguably one of the greatest anthropologists ever, found that Melansian Islanders broke the rules of a ritual when nobody was watching (Malinowski 1922: 30). They took short cuts, trimmed away the corners, and, in short, did what they would dare not do when they were in the company of others. The temptation to go against the accepted norms to advantage oneself, if the occasion allows, is as true of peoples elsewhere as it was of the distant Melansians.

Business Ethics therefore demands that one should function as if one is always in full view. It is hard to say how one would behave if one were completely invisible to others. It is also possible that when one is alone one's private moralities might gain the upper hand over public ethics. It is possible that an individual's morality might favour absolute deference to age, yet this might go against the norms of corporate ethics where achievement counts more than chronological seniority.

Business Ethics works best when you are happy, comfortable and content to be in a fish bowl—transparently in the full view of your stakeholders.

CHAPTER TWO

HOW TO MAKE IT WORK

Putting Business Ethics in Place

The What and Why of Business Ethics

Business Ethics promotes good business by generating significant support structures within the organization as well as outside it. As we have seen, Business Ethics functions on a stakeholder theory of entrepreneurship. The significant stakeholders in any Business Ethics programme are the shareholders, workers, managers, customers, dealers and creditors. In short, stakeholders comprise all those who share a 'legitimate interest' in the firm (Donaldson and Preston 1995: 65–91).

Business Ethics adds value because its effects are felt both within the organization as also among significant stakeholders, such as customers, who are outside it. Internally, a Business Ethics programme promotes sustainable creativity among, and commitment from, workers and management. Externally, complying with Business Ethics helps the company relate better to its customers, its dealers, and to the social and physical environment. Together this allows an enterprise to project itself favourably to all its stakeholders. Without such an endorsement businesses today are severely constrained in realizing their potential.

Business Ethics emerged in the corporate world in response to the fast changing conditions under which enterprises must function in modern times. Customers are more demanding, skilled professionals more exacting, and there is an overall social insistence that businesses observe norms of civic responsibility.

A Business Ethics compliance system ensures that:

1. Workers and management in an organization understand the mission and vision of the company;

2. Both upstream and downstream communication between levels and functions is wired optimally;
3. The company gets appropriate feedback from its customers, dealers and creditors to consolidate its future growth plans; and
4. The company benefits financially from the support provided by it to its social and physical environment.

A Checklist for Business Ethics

An organization is committed to Business Ethics when it has the following:

1. Vision/Mission Statements;
2. Core Values;
3. Business Practice Policy;
4. Code of Conduct;
5. Grievance Counselling Mechanism; and
6. Ethical Dilemma Resolution Workshops.

Needless to say, these have to be arrived at with the full support of the top executives and by engaging executives, managers and subordinate staff in sustained dialogical sessions.

Vision Statement

The vision statement is an extremely important aspect of establishing a Business Ethics process. Very often top executives take it lightly. Consequently they pack the vision statements with high-sounding words that mean little to people working in the organization. The vision statement must be carefully drafted for that is the first and crucial chapter of an ethics document. If it appears to be flamboyant or frivolous, if it gives the appearance of not engaging serious thought and discussion, then the entire document runs the risk of being viewed with utter cynicism.

The vision statement states clearly 'Who We Want to Be.' Do we want to be the biggest manufacturer of denim cloth, or we want to be the most exclusive clothier, or we want to make drugs that are the cutting edge of research, or we want *The vision statement states clearly 'Who We Want to Be.'* to have the best after-sales service available in the engineering industry. We have to make up our minds on this very deliberately and carefully. We must weigh our strengths and weaknesses, keep in touch with the potentials available to us, read the market diligently and then realistically assess the organizational ambitions of the top executives. The vision statement must initially flow out of the highest deliberative body within the firm, and then subjected to feedbacks from others down the line. Only then we can attain a focused and coordinated cooperation in a corporation (see Coase 1937).

Core Values

Crafting core values of the organization is the next step. These core values detail how the vision is to be realized. It spells out: 'How We Do Things Around Here.' To be able to realize who we want to be, we must be very clear about how to get there. Once again there must be careful consideration of these core values. Examples of core values are: impartiality, technical excellence, professional respect between co-workers, or faithful obedience to the law of the land.

General Business Practice

These core values have to be clearly operationalized in terms of general business practice, or official procedure. Each office procedure, whether relating to hiring, rationalizing, reporting wrongdoing, applying for leave, or availing of vacation privileges, must synergize with the core values. The synergy between them must be spelt out. If the core value is to root out nepotism in the organization, then it is important to spell out what exactly constitutes nepotism, and how job hiring will take place so that nepotism is not encouraged. Likewise, if a core value is professional respect then that must be abided by even when rationalizing a firm, deciding on rewards, or planning training programmes.

Code of Conduct

The company's code of conduct is a very important instrument for aligning vision and mission ideals with routine activities. Hence this needs to be crafted very carefully. Here a paradigm shift is strongly recommended, for codes of conduct are usually understood as instruments of coercion and discipline. That of course is true, but for the code to get the authoritative sanction it deserves it must be devised keeping in mind what *cannot* be done by anybody in the organization, no matter how high or distinguished the person may be. The thrust in the code of conduct should be prohibitive in character, and these rules should apply to all without fear or favour.

(a) What Cannot Be Done

The code of conduct must be in synergy with the core values in the mission statement. If the core values have the acceptance of the members of the organization, then the code of conduct automatically gains authority. As the entire ethics process is led by example from the top, the code of conduct should list very clearly what will *not* be tolerated at any cost. Only those aspects should figure in the code of conduct which the top management are confident would be abided by everybody. Any violation of the code would then brook no excuse.

It might seem surprising, but being clear about what *cannot* be done, no matter what the circumstances, tells you a lot about what *can* be done. It has the added benefit of enhancing teamwork and mutual understanding within an organization. A little introspection will tell you that in every walk of life, from the domestic sphere, to sports, to friendships, *don'ts* always come before the *dos*. So why should this not work for the corporate world as well?

> *Being clear about what cannot be done, tells you a lot about what can be done.*

If everybody in the company knows what will not be tolerated no matter who does it, it clears the air and makes working together less prone to confusions and acrimony. Arbitrariness and favouritism find no room in such a regimen, as everybody is equal in terms of the don'ts.

It is now up to the senior management to devise the don'ts of a company as clearly as possible. Care should be taken to play well within one's limits, and not set standards that the chief executive officer too may find difficult to observe.

Once the prohibitions are in place, any contravention of these norms should be consistently acted upon without fear or prejudice. Everybody, from the highest to the lowest, is equal as far as the don'ts are concerned. Only then can the don'ts be metabolized within the rank and file of the organization.

Care must, however, be taken not to *trivialize* this list of don'ts. Further, to maximize the efficacy of the don'ts of an organization, frequent workshops and reviews need to be held. This will help to establish ethical benchmarks and also allow the management to update the list of don'ts. In some cases a few entries may seem superfluous, and in others, perhaps new ones need to be added. Remember, the ethics audit should keep in touch with changing realities and should not assume a life of its own that does not pay attention to the nature of the firm, and the pressing realities outside (see Power 1994, 1997).

Finally, even to be flexible one needs to know what cannot be done. In order to be flexible there must be a frame, and the list of don'ts provides just that. Without this frame that constrains, every arbitrary conduct can aspire to pass off as flexibility. Why give an opening of this sort at all?

Once we are clear on the don'ts, the dos will come by much more easily and effectively.

(b) The Commandments in the Code of Conduct

Contrast the Ten Commandments with the eight-fold path of Buddhism and what is the first thing that strikes you? The Ten Commandments are worded negatively in terms of 'thou shalt not' while the Buddhist imperatives are worded positively. In Buddhism the censor is within, but Christianity provides objective and verifiable criteria for judging the faithful.

Buddhism emphasizes inner states and worldly renunciation, while Christianity insists that those who belong to the faith submit more readily to external authority in matters of religious doctrine and approved conduct. Does this make Christianity more amenable to material pursuits that require collective participation? Can this trait corroborate somewhat the general conclusion among social historians that of all religious persuasions, Christianity is the most conducive to modern corporate enterprise?

The Ten Commandments need not be just a biblical doctrine confined only to those who are declared Christians. The corporate world can take a cue from the format of the Ten Commandments, especially in the crafting of a code of conduct. Just as the Ten Commandments clearly spell out what is forbidden for everybody, so also it is necessary for a corporate code of conduct to unambiguously list what cannot be permitted.

A code of conduct works best when it is not prescriptive, but prohibitive, in character. This makes it easier to monitor wrongdoings. Better still, it allows the corporate executive to know the limits and saves a lot of valuable time in debating over 'should I or should I not'. While it is not necessary that there should be exactly

10 injunctions in the code of conduct, they should all be framed in a 'thou shalt not' style.

A code of conduct framed negatively provides no excuse for shortcuts and pressures business managers and executives to think more creatively. Anyone with years of experience will vouch that the easy way and the shortcut yield short-term benefits but are harmful in the long run. They do not breed talent and genuine expertise.

A code of conduct framed negatively will provide no excuse for shortcuts and force executives to think more creatively.

It is not as if the Ten Commandments are a stand-alone product framed in a bygone and mythical era of human history. The spirit of the Ten Commandments can be seen even today in the rules for sport. Cricket umpires are not chosen for their skill at the game, but are judged on the basis of how well they know the rules, and if they can effectively intervene when a player does something wrong.

An umpire never gives a batsman out for an excellent stroke down the carpet to the boundary. Has any football referee given a yellow or red card to a player who kicks the balls superbly into the net? It is only when there is clarity on what cannot be done, that people excel in their chosen profession. You would not have a Tendulkar or a Pele or a Michael Jordan, if cricket, football or basketball did not have strict rules making clear what a player cannot do no matter how tempting the circumstances.

Not always are rules of sport unambiguous; they too evolve in their search for clarity. Over time new tensions and practices emerge which had not been anticipated.

These issues, when not addressed effectively, are likely to spoil the temper of the game, perhaps irrevocably. Today, sledging (or verbal abuse) in cricket has become a controversial matter. Sledging was not widespread in the past, and hence there was no explicit ruling on this. Now that it is common, clarity is called for. Without this, players, spectators and sport officials will all entertain a diversity of views on this subject. This cannot be good for the game. Without a clear ruling on this matter, before long an ugly incident may happen on the field.

The rules of sport are akin to ethical norms. They inform relations between competitors and between players in the team. Business Ethics too brings out the best in the corporate world by unambiguously prescribing what cannot be done. This principle also goes by the term 'transparency' in corporate argot. The second rule of Business Ethics is to succeed. Put the two together and we have a match-winning combination on our side. Winning may not be everything, but is certainly better than coming second best.

There is nothing unethical in striving to win. In fact, without this drive ethics would be almost unrealizable. Imagine two teams playing to lose. No rule in the world would apply in such conditions. It is only when teams agree that one of them must win that ethics comes into its own. Rules are laid out, spectators get drawn in, even ancillary industries sprout up to fuel the competition. Ethics is clearly for Type A personalities, who play hard and play to win.

Ethics is clearly for Type A personalities, who play hard and play to win.

As Business Ethics is about winning by the rules it brings out entrepreneurial initiatives like nothing else can. As everything is public and out in the open, there is no room now for backroom bargaining or illicit deals. After all, no sporting team has ever won in the dressing room. When such events are repeatedly fixed they degenerate into a farce, like professional wrestling of today. It is then no longer a sport but a carnival.

To succeed in sports is to succeed under public gaze. It is imperative therefore that the rules of the game be thoroughly internalized. In business too the only solution to ethical dilemmas is to know by reflex what not to do at any cost. A quick resolution of such dilemmas frees the mind to engage in the adventure of enterprise. If sanctions for breaking rules are not negotiable, so also the rewards for winning by the rules come with no strings attached, and with no reason to conceal.

Business Ethics emphasizes team spirit, which is just as well. Given the exigencies of the contemporary corporate world, it is impossible to win alone. Today competition is tough because technological information is widely disseminated. In such a situation it is imperative that the team pull together and individual members self-consciously refrain from grandstanding on their own. As the ethical rules of business are unyielding for all, it is worth remembering that the banana that leaves the bunch is the one that gets skinned.

When a code of conduct is articulated clearly in terms of what can never be permitted, then it also helps in taking decisions as to how exceptions are to be made in office rules. There are rules for taking leave, entering expenses, travelling, and so forth. These rules should not be confused with a code of conduct for these have a different concern. These are general business principles which are prescriptive in character. These are in the nature of how to do something.

Even so, from time to time, an exception has to be made with respect to a certain rule. Every business executive is familiar with such occasions. But how are such exceptions to be made? Is there a rule for breaking a rule?

Here again the code of conduct is very relevant. Exceptions can be made only if they do not violate the code of conduct. For instance, if the code of conduct says that the integrity of accounts cannot be tampered with, then that has to be observed even if the amount involved is trivial! Likewise, an employee who teaches school-children, or does social work after office hours, must declare that there is no monetary advantage to be gained from such pursuits. This would make it clear to all that the code of conduct forbidding any other employment is not being violated.

A code of conduct is therefore a useful ally on a number of occasions but it works best when it is written in stone by the burning bush and in the thicket of experience. Only then can it resolve dilemmas and promote true excellence.

The Inescapability of Business Ethics

So if an organization is keen to set up explicit norms that will guide its general business principles and code of conduct, it has little option but to craft a *business ethics manual*. Such a manual will begin with the vision statement and proceed from there to a limpid declaration of actual norms, practices and what the company considers to be strict *no-nos*. A good ethics manual will integrate these different aspects within a common and reiterative scheme so that the whole manual hangs together as a unity. This is what professional executives appreciate the most. An ethics manual is good and convincing when the lowest level employee in the organization can make sense of it and explain it to an outsider in much the same way as the top executive does.

Understood in this fashion, Business Ethics comes through as a practical and hardy management instrument. This is what makes for its greater receptivity among executives. All executives, quite rightly, adopt a 'prove it to me' stance whenever a managerial suggestion comes their way. Business Ethics is, therefore, not just an end in itself. It is, very significantly, also a means towards realizing corporate targets.

The fact that Business Ethics is an eminently practical way of going about doing business has often been lost sight of because the meaning of ethics itself has not been properly understood. Once ethics is pegged to the conception of the 'other' then not only must the ethical principles be dialogically realized, their effects must also be positive and *objectively demonstrable*. This should take care of the concern voiced by many that to adopt ethics in business cripples the efficacy of the organization and makes it less competitive. In fact, when Business Ethics is comprehensively practiced it has just the opposite effect. It releases initiative and commitment from different categories of managers and staff within the organization, thereby increasing the overall efficiency of the enterprise.

While many unethical enterprises can do well in the short run, Business Ethics kicks in for the long distance runner.

While many unethical enterprises can do well in the short run, Business Ethics kicks in for the long distance runner: the marathon performer. In the long run only the ethical survive— neither luck nor patronage can be depended upon as their influences are extremely vulnerable to time. Do corporate houses in India appreciate that? Yes, they are beginning to, but there is still a lot of ground to be covered. Much will depend on how quickly we are able to demonstrate the practical side of Business Ethics and cleanse it of its many misleading connotations.

The Last Piece of Cake

The most effective policies are those that are procedurally just. For example, if the person cutting the cake knows that the last piece will be his, this will automatically ensure that all slices will be of equal size. As the procedure itself is just, its results are not open to contentious disputes. When the person who cuts the cake gets the last slice then everybody, high and low, is assured of a fair deal.

To be able to make this principle work in the corporate sector it is necessary for senior management to imaginatively adopt the perspective of those who are less privileged than they are within the organization. Such a strategy should not be confused with populism or working class syndicalism. It is, in fact, good management practice.

While formulating mission statements and codes of conduct it is necessary, therefore, for senior executives to imagine themselves occupying positions that are subordinate to their own. This process needs to be worked down the line, methodically and step by step. It may come as a surprise to policymakers what a difference such a

Senior managers need to imagine themselves in the positions of their subordinates.

perspective immediately brings about. Many wrong perceptions about one another are cleared in this process. This strategy has the further advantage of arousing empathy at all levels. As Konusuka Matsushita, the legendary chairman of Matsushita Electrical and Industrial Company, advised, the leader should spend 70 per cent of the time in building on the positive qualities of the subordinates, and only 30 per cent in correcting their faults (Matsushita 1996: 71).

It is not as if all distinctions, privileges, and perks are being removed or equalized. This process only enlivens the appreciation of the conditions that others work in and of their legitimate ambitions. These include professional respect, scope for upward mobility, and an unbiased regimen of rewards and sanctions. No matter at which level people are, it is necessary for a baseline similarity among all employees. Only then can it be said that they work for the company and not just in the company.

To keep the competitive juices flowing, frills can and must be added later on. But the extent of frills will depend on how much is left over once the policy of realizing substantive equalities is met. It's not as if those at the top first help themselves to hefty slices of the cake and leave only crumbs for officials and employees at lower levels.

Once top executives and members of the senior management hypothetically put themselves in the positions of those who are not quite as privileged as they are, they need to ask themselves some very simple questions. These questions need to be consistently raised at every organizational tier within the company. What would I do if I were in this post? What are the basic job insecurities at this level? How can I advance in my career to a more senior position? What other facilities could I enjoy which would make my work more productive and less of a drudgery? Last, but not least, do people in my company respect me for my work?

In order to raise these issues with empathy it is necessary for those at the top to assume that they are behind a veil (Rawls 1971). It is as if they do not quite know which position they would occupy once the veil is lifted. It is from behind this veil that they should formulate codes of conduct, business conduct documents, and mission statements. When senior executives follow this method and keep these issues in mind, the organizational rules they eventually arrive at will appear more just. These rules will carry greater conviction down the line.

The advantage of adopting this procedure is that there is a fusion of diverse perspectives. Those who formulate mission statements and codes of conduct have, by virtue of their experience and training, a more comprehensive grasp of the competitive status of the company they work for. When they go behind the veil they do not leave behind this vision. In fact they put it to the test by imaginatively placing themselves in a hypothetical situation at each of the significant levels in their company.

But every cake needs an icing. Thus far the documents are still somewhat unfinished. It is necessary to take the further step and review them with other members of the organization. Once that is accomplished, business conduct documents and mission statements are ready to go to work. What's more, they get better with usage. You can at last eat your cake and have it too.

The Importance of Synergy

The entire exercise in Business Bthics must proceed logically, step by step. There should be a close and intimate relationship between each of the sections in an ethics document, and every effort should be made to spell out the synergy between core values and general business principles and code of conduct. This will help in the resolution of ethical dilemmas as well. As ethical dilemmas are a very important aspect of an ethical process we will return to that separately a little later.

To sum up:

A clearly spelt out ethical business process would emphasize *synergies* between:

1. Vision Statement;
2. Mission Statement;
3. Core Values;
4. General Business Principles; and
5. Code of Conduct.

For example, consider the schematic representation below:

Core Value	Policy	Demonstrated Effect	Key Indicator
Impartiality	Hiring policy	Quality recruits	Increase in skilled personnel
Transparency	No discretionary payments	Greater stress on quality	Per cent fall in miscellaneous expenses
Professional respect	Objective criteria for evaluation	Skills upgraded	On job rise in qualifications
Accountability	Take responsibility for success and failure	Greater team work	Fall in grievances reported

Each of the entries under the headers core value, policy, demonstrated effect and key indicator, is only by way of illustration. What is important is that each of these vertical columns must be completed in a coherent fashion to give empirical substance to the variables listed horizontally. Such a synergic exercise would objectively demonstrate why good ethics is good business and would rally the primary stakeholders behind the company in a participatory fashion.

As we have been emphasizing all along, for a Business Ethics programme to succeed, the effects should be easily demonstrable. Top executives should consistently strain to objectify core values so that these norms gain in authority and all stakeholders see their worth. This test is very critical, for at the end of the day, this is what separates ethics from morality.

Prioritizing Values

We now need to return to the making of a company's mission statement. As we have suggested, only the relevant core values should be included in it. Now a further point needs to be emphasized. These core values have to be prioritized.

Many business houses in India are disappointed that their high-sounding mission statements just do not work. These statements say all the right things, with the appropriate degree of gravity, and yet fail to generate corporate enthusiasm. This has given the impression, at least in some quarters, that a mission statement is all about getting dressed up with nowhere to go.

To get the most out of a mission statement it is not as if all that is noble and virtuous must be included. The core

values in a mission statement must be limited to those
that are relevant to the organization concerned. But this
is only the beginning. These core values need further
working upon. They have to be prioritized in order of
importance. Without an ordering of this sort it is impossible to communicate mission statements with a straight
face. To love them all equally is reckless promiscuity
even in corporate affairs. It reveals a lack
of seriousness and an unwillingness to
walk the talk.

*A company's core
values need to be
prioritized in order
of importance.*

The sequencing of core values should be
such that only after the first principle is
observed the next gets active, and so
forth down the line. Prioritizing means that latter order
values are articulated and operationalized in terms of
those that precede them. Such an exercise immediately
converts a mission statement into a rugged tool that is
ready for work.

The lesson then is to order, by hierarchy, and prioritize
the core values in a mission statement. For example the
core values of Disney's theme parks are, in order of importance, 'safety', 'courtesy', the 'show', and last of all,
'efficiency' (Blanchard 1998: 33). As 'safety' comes before
all else, parents know that no matter how gravity defy-
ing the rides may appear, their children are safe in a
Disney park.

Imagine for a moment how horrifying Disney parks
would be if the corporation's core values were prioritized differently. If, for instance, the 'show' were more
important than 'safety', a chance accident could ruin
Disney's reputation beyond repair. Or, if 'safety',
'courtesy' and the 'show' were all placed horizontally
at the same level, then the implicit tendency would be
to trade off one for the other on the basis of probability.

A rare statistic of misfortune would be ignored in favour of pushing up profit margins. This would again undermine the 'safety' principle and could mire the enterprise forever.

By prioritizing 'safety', and placing it even above the 'show', Disney has challenged its competitors to rise to higher levels of customer satisfaction. It has set new standards of corporate management in the entertainment industry. This has helped Disney stay well ahead of its competitors. The difference, simply put, is that Disney has a clear idea of how to operationalize its core values and that its prioritization is customized to meet the contingent specifics of theme park entertainment.

Japan's Seven-Eleven stores also have a similar attitude with regard to their core corporate values. They give the highest priority to customer feedback and mould their operations to cater swiftly to customer wants. When the enterprise found that the Japanese have a special yen for fresh food, the Seven-Elevens came up with four deliveries a day. Undaunted by received wisdom on profit generation, this strategy paid off. The market base of Seven-Eleven expanded from the predictable housewives to include students and high-earning members of the salariat. Eventually, Japan's Seven-Eleven stores became so powerful that it bought out its parent US organization, the Southland Corporation. It is now a wholly Japanese affair.

A hierarchical ordering of a company's core values thus helps to focalize entrepreneurial activity in clear and unambiguous terms. Additionally, such a prioritization is crucial for sorting out ethical dilemmas promptly, and without the usual heartburn. No more wringing of hands, or acrimonious pointing of fingers. Moreover, a clearly sequenced mission statement gives an organization its distinctive trait and makes it stand out from the rest. This raises a company's brand equity, as its varied stakeholders now have something tangible to rally around.

Forget the 'Weight Test'

Finally, it is very important not to shoot yourself in the foot in the mistaken belief that a Business Ethics document must be very weighty and cumbersome to arouse awe and obedience. This is the best way to undo all the hard work. A Business Ethics document, or manual, should be user-friendly and easy to handle. A bulky, wordy document is the last thing you need. Consider the following from the world of law.

In contrast to judgements by Indian courts, which run into hundreds of pages, American judgements are very short. Some of the most sensational, landmark judgements in the US have *not* been more than a dozen pages or so. This is probably why law enforcement is so much better there than here. In fact one can confidently pronounce that there is a strong inverse relationship between word and deed.

This lesson should not be lost on the corporate sector. There is a great temptation among some leading firms to demonstrate their zeal for Business Ethics by putting out weighty manuals with long explanations. While this may impress shareholders, and this is not a minor consideration, it does not really work with the employees and management of the company. They get bogged down in details and the purpose behind these manuals is substantially lost.

For ethics manuals to be effective they have to be precise and operational. Ethics manuals are meant primarily for employees and for management of a company. They must be clear on the norms that should govern their interactions within and outside the company. The manuals cannot say everything but should provide guidelines for action based on a few firm principles. To make these manuals effective and translatable in a variety of situations it is important to hold workshops every now and again at regular intervals. But the written document itself should be tightly formulated and precisely articulated.

Let us return again to our analogy with court judgements. Long judgements by Indian courts create fresh ambiguities and contentions, as they do not limit themselves strictly to matters of law. They contain large chunks of moralizing, and, often, a potted history on the subject. In contrast, court judgements in America are precise. The verdicts, in such instances, are framed without extraneous details and with minimum flourish. This is why Lord Halsbury wrote in the preface of his monumental forty-volume work on the laws of England: 'The more words there are, the more words are there about which doubts can be entertained.'

Vision and mission statements should be precise and clearly worded in everyday language.

Corporate leaders should take note of this factor when they work on their ethics manuals. It is very important that the vision and mission statements are clearly worded in *everyday language*. Employees and managers who have to work with this document will be much more positively inclined towards ethical conduct if they have a document that works and not one that sounds bombastic. In fact, the latter induces cynicism because nobody can really be that good!

The next step in a Business Ethics manual should be to connect the vision and mission statements with the basic norms that the company upholds. These norms could be of impartiality, of professional respect, of transparency, and so on. But here again, there should be no cluttering and the list should not be long. These norms should be clearly linked in turn to operational procedures. For example, how is impartiality made effective in job hiring? Or, how is professional respect manifested in knowledge management and training? Or, how is transparency made to work not just in accounting procedures, but in everyday matters from misusing office facilities to punctuality?

It needs to be recognized, particularly in the Indian context, that our tendency is to overwhelm others with words. This is how we are trained from school upwards. Students are encouraged to write more in order to get better marks. Our politicians are known to give very long speeches that amount to nothing. Our courts hand out long judgements that are then disputed over by wrangling lawyers.

Unlike other realms of life where perhaps the taste of the pudding does not lie in its eating, but in its making, the corporate sector has to demonstrate that it is practical and efficient in every department. Those are the only standards by which enterprises will be judged both by their competitors and by their customers. A lot of preparation in terms of workshops, discussions, and brainstorming can go into the making of an ethics manual, but the ultimate product has to be sleek and user-friendly. Being wordy, in such instance, will just not do.

The ethics manual should be portable and handy and should not compete for space with the lunch box in the brief case.

CHAPTER THREE

STEP BY STEP

Guidelines for Business Ethics in Practice

Why Do It?

- To make sure that the organization holds a leadership position in the eyes of the public.
- To increase the intellectual capital of its employees.
- To bring about greater corporate integrity and transparency at all levels.
- To institute a system that binds every functionary of the organization into an ethical unit.
- To resolve ethical dilemmas in accordance with company values.

For a Distinctive Culture

To put in place a Business Ethics system a thorough workshop must be conducted. There is little point in lifting a Business Ethics manual from some organization, tampering with it, paraphrasing it in parts, and hoping it will work in your company as well. If the top management is serious about Business Ethics then it should seriously work towards a customized ethics manual of its own that will guide how the ethics system should operate, from the mission statement to the code of conduct to ethical dilemmas.

In other words the Business Ethics system must address the issue of creating a specific company culture to which all executives, managers and employees will feel a strong sense of attachment. A corporate unit is not just a site where profits are made, and jobs are performed, it is also a culture-producing unit. In order to consolidate a distinctive culture a

A corporate unit is not just a site where profits are made, and jobs are performed, it is also a culture-producing unit.

company obviously cannot lift a Business Ethics manual and procedure from somewhere else and hope it will work in a different set of circumstances.

To address this dimension of creating a distinctive culture the following concerns must be adequately attended to:

(i) To create symbols with which employees at all levels can identify with and commit themselves to. This can be achieved in a variety of ways. For example:

- The company could see itself as a technological leader in the field.
- The company could take pride in being a humane organization by, for instance, having the best medical and retirement policy.
- The company could also draw advantage from its customer and after-sales service.
- The functionaries of the company could also see themselves as custodians of society's conscience.

(This is only by way of illustration. The creation of symbolic identification will have to be done keeping in mind the specifics of the company concerned).

(ii) To self-consciously establish criteria that would distinguish the organization concerned from other organizations, particularly with respect to other enterprises in the same field or industry. It can do so by:

- Drawing, from the symbols established above, those features that separate it from other concerns.

- Making the training and recruitment procedure one that makes the selected feel more exclusive.
- Openly declaring its allegiance to ethical procedures.
- Giving the employees a stake in the organization's functioning.
- Institutionalizing benefits and sanctions that are common to employees at all levels.

The Ethics Metric as the First Step

Before the actual workshop begins, it is very important to first assess the status of the organization concerned on the *ethics metric*.

- Can an ordinary employee explain the organization's mission statement?
- Does the organization have clear rules on what is not acceptable practice at any cost?
- Has the organization set up a system of red flags in critical areas?
- Is there an office of ombudsman in the organization?
- How does the organization take into account employment grievances?
- Are there systems by which whistle-blowers are encouraged and protected?
- How does the company take advantage of employee suggestions and initiatives?
- Does the organization's code of conduct emerge from discussions across levels and functions?
- Is there an independent, periodic audit of code of conduct, business practices, etc?

- What steps has the company taken to evolve a specific culture of its own?
- How does the company align its products or services with dominant social concerns?
- In what ways does the organization measure its customers' perception of its functioning?
- Does the organization have a process for optimizing stakeholders' interests by conducting dealership, creditor and customer reviews?

An assessment based on the above is important, for it will then serve as a comparative framework against which to judge the implementation and effects of an ethics programme.

Resolving Ethical Dilemmas

One of the most critical aspects of a Business Ethics workshop is to design a way of resolving persistent ethical dilemmas. Business Ethics goes well beyond recommending that we obey the law. It also helps us to take a stand when we are faced with ethical dilemmas. In recent years there has been a greater appreciation of this issue, across industries, probably because of the many financial and white-collar crimes that have shaken the corporate world internationally. Consequently, there is a growing body of opinion among corporate executives that if ethical dilemmas were handled appropriately at the right time then that would perhaps have prevented full-scale frauds from taking place.

Ethical dilemmas are *shades of grey.* Unlike legal issues, which are in black and white, ethical dilemmas are not expressly against the law but need to be handled correctly and collectively. If left unattended they can create legal problems in the not too distant future. Let us take some typical ethical dilemmas: Does your company have a policy on giving and receiving gifts? If not, then it is high time such a policy is framed. If your travel agent offers you a deal which does not hurt company coffers but goes against company policy, then what should you do? It is surprising how often such a dilemma faces management and staff in many organizations. Or, if your dealer offers, with no strings attached, admission to your son in a school of your choice, what should be your response? Or, when your relation is an aspirant for a job, should you do a) tell your superiors about it, b) keep quiet, c) stay away from the recruitment process, or d) actively discourage the relation? A tough choice, this one, particularly in the context of the Indian family. All these issues are ethical dilemmas and each company must find the right responses for them by conducting periodic workshops. We shall take up this aspect for discussion in a more detailed fashion in the *Appendix* to this chapter when we address the issue of ethical dilemma workshops.

Ethical dilemmas, if left unattended, can create legal problems.

Workshop at Work

While there is no off-the-shelf Business Ethics manual, the best way of putting a customized Business Ethics system in place is through conducting workshops. In the following pages we present a schematic sequencing of the various stages of a Business Ethics workshop to make the process easy to comprehend.

Stages

(i) Orientation.
(ii) Interactive Participation.
(iii) Management Interventions.
(iv) Consolidation.
(v) Continuous Evaluation.

Stage I

Orientation (Phase I): Felt Needs' Assessment

The principal thrust at this stage is to get a nuanced sense of how the department heads and selected senior managers have actually experienced dilemmas and anxieties on these issues. As the actual experiences will have several variations it will help in concretizing themes that will be later discussed in the workshop.

The assessment of felt needs is very different from usual surveys. Categories will emerge in this case from actual experiences as related by the participants. As far as possible all preconceived ideas should be kept in suspension till inputs are received from the personnel who will be involved at this stage. This is necessary so that the authenticity of responses and the vivacity of personal/subjective valuations are not compromised by prefixed grids of data analysis.

A major feature of this stage is to convince the participants of the importance of paying attention to the human dimensions of corporate work, and how considerations of integrity and ethics are eminently practical concerns (see also pages 22–25). In other words, besides eliciting the felt needs of the departmental heads and the senior managers, a concurrent purpose is to win their buy-in as well.

The personnel involved at this stage will be the departmental heads and selected senior managers.

Orientation (Phase II): Pilot Study

In this second phase of the orientation stage a pilot study will be designed after assessing the responses of senior management and of a representative sample from different levels and functions within the organization. In this pilot study a workshop-like situation will be simulated but it will be done on an individual basis and not involve group interaction. This phase is necessary so that the final module for the workshop does not suffer from any communication gaps, nor does it give rise to contradictory interpretations of the themes that will be slated for deliberations. This pilot study is essentially in the nature of a dummy run to iron out possible errors and omissions in the final workshop module.

Stage II: Interactive Participation

Activity	Workshop (time period is variable)
	Combined sessions
	Panel sessions on selected themes
Personnel involved	Total not more than 50–60, including
	Executive heads
	Senior managers
	Selected junior managers

Purpose I (Fact-Finding)

Quite obviously, it is necessary to conduct a fact-finding exercise on the influence of explicit and implicit ethics process, and the expectations and perceptions of senior executives and junior staff on management and work-related issues. This information will be many-layered as it will be made up of inputs from participants at different levels, and also because they will be asked to respond to important organizational issues that came up in the earlier stages of investigation with executives and managers in a less structured setting.

Purpose II (Resolving Ethical Dilemmas)

A special session must be held to address the various ethical dilemmas that the organization faces at various levels and what the various responses to them are. The workshop should enable the participants to agree on some common responses to ethical dilemmas, keeping in mind the synergies between mission statement and norms of functioning within the organization. A sample of the section on ethical dilemmas is attached as *Appendix* to this chapter.

Interactive Participation

In this phase first a *preliminary report* ought to be prepared for departmental heads and some concerned senior managers. Whether individually or jointly, or out of a mix of the two, feedbacks to the report will be solicited.

With the help of this further input from *dialogical interaction* over the preliminary report, a *final report* will be worked upon. This final report will fine-tune the pre-liminary report and make it immediately translatable in terms of management interventions.

The *final report* will contain, first, a factual morphology of the concrete issues that the company is concerned with. It will not simply be a break-up of responses in percentage terms, but will provide qualitative and *thick* descriptive interpretations of how dilemmas, anxieties and prospects are viewed from the managerial-level upwards.

This will form the base of the concrete recommendations for executive interventions, which will constitute the second part of our *final report*.

Stage III: Management Intervention

There will probably be two categories of interventions: *initiative and remedial.*

Initiative recommendations will be of the kind that the company will need to institute afresh to take care of a set of problem areas that will be detailed alongside.

Remedial recommendations will be of the kind that would suggest alternative modalities of performing existing functions and activities. These suggestions will provide ways of enhancing focus, or suggesting new foci in order to help recast what is already being done, with practices and personnel already in place. Both these types of recommendations will be with the aim of enhancing corporate integrity and raising the social profile of the company.

Stage IV: Consolidation

In this stage the initiatives set in by the company on the basis of the workshop and report will be consolidated. This will be done by monitoring the consequences of recommended managerial interventions across levels and functions. This stage will culminate with the establishment of an Integrity and Ethical Benchmark. This benchmark will help to monitor and evaluate the functioning of the company over a period of time. Should there be a fall then it can be quickly detected before any lasting damage takes place.

In order to establish this benchmark discussions and meetings will have to be held with departmental heads, and selected senior and junior managers.

Stage V: Continuous Evaluation: Benchmarking and Ombudsman

This next stage is to enable the concern to build in the inputs from the previous stages on a permanent basis. This stage will again review the status of the recommended management interventions and their strategic effects. A benchmark study will also be included at this time.

Benchmarking

Benchmarking is a serious affair and should be given a lot of consideration. The recommended way to benchmark would be to stay close to the following format. First identify your stakeholders carefully and then

disaggregate them. For each category of relevant stakeholder, such as employee, customer, dealer, etc., identify
the dominant area of concern. These will differ across
stakeholders, though there will be overlaps. After this
is done, then key performance indicators need to be
identified with a clear specification of who the responsible officer is in each instance. For example, if the stakeholders are the community then perhaps the area of
concern might be noise pollution, or overcrowding, or
the need for local employment. If the stakeholder is the
customer, then the area of concern may be after-sales
service. Then customer satisfaction on after-sales service
needs to be ascertained, and should the levels of satisfaction fall below an identified threshold, then the
relevant authority to address the problem should be
specified. The same could be repeated with the employees as stakeholders, or creditors as stakeholders. It
is important that one does not overlook which officials
and departments are responsible for the satisfactory
ratings on each of the key performance indicators.

Schematically then:

Identify Stakeholder	Area of concern	Key Performance Indicators	Relevant Authority

This exercise is essential for the continuous evaluation
of the ethics process and should be conducted in tandem
with the suggestion on ethical synergies in Chapter 2.

Ombudsman

The office of the ombudsman is also very significant for
the purposes of continuous evaluation. It provides the
node for periodic assessment of the company's status

in terms of integrity and ethics. While different officials at different levels and branches in the organization may be directly responsible for addressing stakeholders' grievances, the ombudsman's office can ideally provide the kind of coordination and record maintenance that is necessary for the purposes of continuous evaluation.

In addition, the ombudsman's office allows employees the benefit of discussing their problems and airing their suggestions to an impartial but concerned third party. It is most important that the confidentiality of the employees be protected by the ombudsman. It will be the job of the ombudsman to collate and systematize the outcome of these interactions with employees at all levels and pass them on for executive consideration.

The ombudsman will not adjudicate disputes, nor directly implement suggestions. As a third party the ombudsman will work towards maintaining and enhancing the company's status on the ethical benchmark scale on a continuous basis.

For continuous evaluation it is recommended that:

- The office of ombudsman be set up.
- Periodic benchmarking takes place to assess the ethical status of the organization.
- It is ensured that the company takes care of its stakeholders by keeping abreast of developments in knowledge, both technical and social.

Stage VI: Giving High Visibility

Finally it is very important for the organization to communicate, to all its stakeholders, the fact that it has a Business Ethics process in place. This can be done through the following:

- Annual Reports.
- Advertisements.
- Organizing seminars and talks.

When you have done the job well, let others know about it. That is how one spreads the good word. That is also how one adds value with the stakeholders.

Appendix to Chapter 3

Ethical Dilemmas Workshop: Some Illustrations

As ethical dilemmas are rarely posed in stark black and white terms, they become extremely tricky and testy. It is easy to reject something that is clearly illegal, or that which immediately inflicts a financial burden on the company. But what if the options present themselves in different shades of grey, as they usually do? It was von Hayek who warned us that personal responsibility has to be exercised keeping in mind an amoral market (von Hayek 1967).

In such situations it is necessary to recognize that there is frequently a lack of fit between the literal meaning of a company norm and the dilemmas of action that a concrete situation may present. This is why it is necessary that codes of conduct and ethical norms be invigorated by discussions on the numerous dilemmas that may emerge out of them. This helps to make all such company documents practical and workable.

There are numerous ethical problems that confront people every day. If the company car is taken for an official trip then under what circumstances can private errands also be entertained in the same round? If an urgent call is to be made to a relative abroad can the company's phone be used after office hours for that purpose? If there are some unconfirmed doubts on the safety of a product then how should the company react — Wait till a final report comes in or initiate proactive steps to investigate into the matter or take the product off the shelf pending an authoritative clarification?

It is not as if such dilemmas must necessarily entail a huge financial loss. Yet a little reflection will show that if clear answers are not provided to problems of this sort then little molehills can become mountains one day.

So before it begins to hurt it is important to accept that ethical dilemmas exist. It is not as if company rules once put down are not open to multiple interpretations and exceptions. It is unreasonable to expect them to be that way. Once this is acknowledged then the only solution is to hold regular ethical workshops. This is the best way to breathe life into company policy.

Ethical Dilemma

Q. If a colleague, who is also a close friend, has been over-heard disclosing confidential financial information to his broker, what would you do:
   a) Tell the person it is not right.
   b) Report to superior.
   c) Ignore it after person admits mistake.
   d) Accept it as none of one's business.
   e) Any other, please specify.

Ethical Dilemma

Q. *A close relation is a potential supplier to the company, what would you do:*
   a) Decide to keep quiet and let the best offer win.
   b) Report to the superior and keep away from negotiations.
   c) Help the relation to become the supplier.
   d) Any other, please specify.

Ethical Dilemma

Q. *A company vehicle has been rented for the day. Would it be used to run some pressing domestic errands?*
   a) Abide strictly by the official routine.
   b) Attend to those errands which are *en route*.
   c) Do both official and domestic work.
   d) Ask superior's permission to run domestic errands as well.
   e) Use the vehicle for domestic chores and tip the driver.
   f) Make an exception only when the domestic chore is very important.
   g) Any other, please specify.

Ethical Dilemma

Q. *A bribe has been demanded to release an imported consignment of goods, what would you do:*
   a) Pay the bribe quickly.
   b) Discuss with superior before taking a decision.
   c) Report the official to higher authorities.
   d) Refuse to pay the bribe.

e) Pay the bribe and think of alternative solutions for the next time.

f) Any other, please specify.

Ethical Dilemma

Q. *Your travel agent offers an economy ticket for self and spouse to go abroad at the price of a full fare ticket that the company purchased, what would you do:*
   a) Take the offer.
   b) Report the matter to your superior.
   c) Refuse the offer.
   d) Refuse the offer and warn the agent.
   e) Any other, please specify.

Ethical Dilemma

Q. *If expensive gifts are received from a subordinate on Diwali, what would you do:*
   a) Take the gift but admonish subordinate.
   b) Take the gift and reciprocate with a gift in return.
   c) Refuse the gift.
   d) Take the gift and place it in the office/Or share it among colleagues.
   e) Any other, please specify.

Ethical Dilemma

Q. *If a supplier offers to have your child admitted to a particular school or college, what would you do:*
   a) Make sure there are no strings tied to the offer.
   b) Refuse his help.
   c) Find out if he can really help or he is just boasting.

d) Take his help but resolve not to be partial towards him.
e) Take his help, for child's career is very important.
f) Any other, please specify.

Ethical Dilemma

Q. *If someone in the company makes a casual disparaging remark about a person's caste or religion, what would you do:*
   a) Laugh it off as a casual remark.
   b) Rebuke the offending colleague.
   c) Report the matter to superior.
   d) Talk to the aggrieved party and decide the best course of action.
   e) Any other, please specify.

CHAPTER FOUR

TOWARDS SUSTAINABILITY

Ethics Driven Corporate Social Responsibility

Globalization and Corporate Social Responsibility

The word 'globalization' defies a precise meaning primarily because it is so enmeshed with ideological considerations—both left and right. Enemies of globalization view it as a legitimizing of insatiable capitalist appetite preying on the world's poor and hungry vulnerable population, while its proponents see it primarily as an agent of bringing prosperity to all (including the hitherto dispossessed) through the agency of the market. Quite apart from partisanship of this sort, it cannot be doubted that globalization has acquired an intellectual presence which is much larger than the politics of the left or the right. It is now a social phenomenon, and not just an ideological label for populist banter.

What makes globalization rise above the din of political wrangle is the fact that there has been a qualitative differ-ence in the way people are beginning to relate to one another. This transition has occurred slowly, and even un-self-consciously. Yet, what cannot be denied is that the emphasis has shifted, more noticeably in developing countries, from producerism to consumerism. Consumerism should not be understood here in a negative fashion, as it usually is in most popular renditions of the term. Instead, it should be seen as an expression of a demotic sentiment that arises among consumers who demand higher standards at all levels, from the commodity they buy, to the ways they are produced, right down to the producer's commitment towards being a corporate citizen.

It is in this context that industries today consider, or should consider, the question of Corporate Social

Responsibility. It is not enough to be philanthropic and not think in terms of consumers and other relevant stakeholders. It is not enough to be law abiding and leave matters at that, for a business rival round the corner can raise the stakes by introducing commodities and services, as well as conditions of production that are much higher than those required by law. Consumers today are alive to these changes and react to them in a fashion that tells on the bottom line of a firm. Therefore, the fact of corporate social responsibility (CSR) has to be carefully devised keeping in mind the specifics of the organization and the kinds of demands that can be made upon it as a corporate citizen by all its relevant stakeholders.

At the same time, no company can afford to let its profits fall. In fact, if that were to happen then it would be letting down its stockholders and employees, who are two of its very important stakeholders. The question then is: how to devise a system of CSR that is related to business so that both can be sustained in synergy.

Friedman's Dilemma

Let me begin with what may be called the 'Friedman Dilemma'. Recall Friedman's influential essay 'Social Responsibility of Business' that we have already referred to in Chapter One. The dilemma Friedman posed was that striving for profit was inimical to chasing social causes as the latter was nothing less than unadulterated socialism. Of course, corporate philanthropy was allowed for, but only after profits were properly secured.

It is true that a firm must make profits in order to survive. It is also true that without profit there is no firm and no corporate social activity. But it is not true that corporate social responsibility is something that comes after profits are made and money deposited with the stockholders. Nor is it true that corporate social responsibility (CSR) is only for the big players and that smaller entrepreneurs have to make their money first.

For Milton Friedman, corporate philanthropy is alright, but anything resembling corporate social responsibility is letting the shareholders down. But CSR is not the same as philanthropy,[1] though most are not clear about the difference. There is no doubt that in a country like India corporate philanthropy has a significant place, but corporate social responsibility, or CSR has a different charter. CSR, at its best, is about the corporate sector reaching out from within the company to the society outside in order to benefit both business and the social and physical environment in which it functions. CSR thus synergises social and business interests, and it is this coupling that makes it different from philanthropy, as we know it to be.

The rub however lies in making CSR sustainable. If CSR has attained a kind of unreal and ethereal reputation it is largely because it is confused with projects that are not driven by business interests but by whims and fancies of the top executives. CSR is not about digging wells and setting up schools and feeding babies. All too often CEOs are smitten by remorse and guilt and want

---

[1] Indeed, 63 per cent of the capital of Tata Sons Ltd. is held by trusts for philanthropic purposes, and it is popular knowledge how effectively the funds of this trust are employed for a variety of purposes, from health to education to building infrastructural facilities.

to do something 'relevant' in the world at large and they call that CSR. In fact, such activities have little to do with CSR, and if anything they resemble corporate philanthropy. Here again, in most cases, the commitment is not long lasting as it is primarily driven by the CEO's personal preferences about which causes to support.

Stakeholder Perspective and CSR

Keeping this in mind, one can now take the next step and argue that corporate social responsibility is best put in practice when it helps meet the expectations of a firm's stakeholders. This implies that CSR must have a business perspective without being obsessed by profits. If one keeps ethics as top priority the bottom line will swell, and swell in a sustainable way. It is true that many have got away by being sheer robber barons in the way they do business, but let it be known that the life of such organizations is very short, and sometimes even the biggest, like Enron, can have a mighty fall.

To make CSR sustainable it is necessary to keep the business interest of the company in mind. If this is not done then CSR programmes will run so long as the top executive is personally involved in it and wither away when something more gripping comes around and grabs the leader's attention. CSR cannot be left to personal whims and fancies, nor should CSR be seen as something that is done as an afterthought once profits have been made. CSR is an aspect of everyday business and executives would do well to see it that way.

All too often one is told that CSR is about obeying the law. This is not correct. Obeying the law is a necessary but not sufficient condition for practicing CSR. Jamsetji Tata made that clear decades ago when he said that if after adherence to the law one does not feel quite correct, then it is necessary to raise our standards even higher. CSR is an evolving concern and quite in keeping with the way in which business is transforming itself on account of a number of factors.

Customers are now much more conscious of standards, stakeholders are aware of their interests, and more than anything else, the co-workers of a company are viewed quite differently from the way they were perceived till a few decades ago. No longer is the boss made in the mould of the tycoon who towered over everyone else with his authority and charisma. Now the top executive is like the captain of a team who is out there to get the best performance possible by energizing the potentialities in each of the players. In this process the boss too strives to be that much better, that much more effective, every day.

Three Models of CSR

Corporate social responsibility must also be in tune with these imperatives and that is why all initiatives on this score must be stakeholder oriented and driven by business interests if they are to be sustainable. Accordingly I propose three models of CSR:

1. Competency Driven
2. Community Driven
3. Consumer Driven

These three models are not hermetically sealed units as there are frequent overlaps between them. Nevertheless, it can be maintained that the area of emphasis is different for each one of them and that is why it is important to separate them analytically.

Competency Driven

In this model of CSR, the company reaches out to the society by depending on its core competencies. In doing so, it helps create potential stakeholders, and also adds to evolving higher efficiency standards. In such instances of CSR, the company delves deep into the firm's core competencies in its corporate outreach. In doing so it finds new areas where its competencies can be manifested and fresh circumstances that challenge its established routine. Put them together and they add up to higher performance levels within the organization as well, providing one is willing to learn.

Examples of such competency driven CSR are many. When Lipton Company in Etah decided to help set up veterinary hospitals in the region from where it gets its milk supplies, it helped the dairy farmers within its area of operation, as well as itself. There was a greater awareness of how to effectively increase milk supplies, and what are the best ways of improving the quality of milch cattle. Excel, an agro-based enterprise took upon itself to recycle garbage in Mumbai and thereby enlarged a new dimension to its core competency besides helping clean the city. Tata Hotels have used their knowledge in food, beverage and room management to help poor people cook nutritious food at lower costs and run rehabilitation homes. Several IT companies have set up computer literacy programmes. Multinational drug companies, like Pfizer, are interested in supporting hospices that challenge their existing competency in drug manufacture.

Community Driven

In community driven CSR, organizations invest in social welfare but with a business interest again. For example, TELCO and Tata Chemicals have created recreational facilities around artificial lakes that are filled with water purified from industrial effluents. By undertaking to enlarge public facilities of this sort, several Tata companies are committed to subscribing to a sustainable form of CSR. IKEA, the Swedish Home Furnishing multi-national, has set up bridge schools in carpet belt areas in east Uttar Pradesh as it sources a lot of material from there. IKEA is committed to keeping units it has business relations with free of child labour. By establishing such schools it tries to create incentives for parents to keep their children away from the job market. At the same time this pressures its suppliers to raise their performance standards. Some IKEA suppliers have been so enthused by this project that they too have set up schools signalling thereby to their workers that they are committed to maintaining high standards of production. Such instances need not just be limited to private companies. Sugar co-operatives in Maharashtra have set up Kolhapur dams to help the farmers that supply sugar cane to them and this has also led co-operatives to be more aware of the technologies of sugar cane production. Some co-operatives have also started schools and technical institutions where the children of small shareholders can be trained and later absorbed in the organisation's work force.

Consumer Oriented

It is now widely recognized that consumer pressure has made a great difference in sensitizing companies to the needs of stakeholders. But what must be acknowledged in addition is that CSR can also help in raising consumer standards and expectations. In this process not only is the consumer benefited, but the company too can hike up the competition in its own market sector. For example, if a cloth producing company insists that it will purchase cotton only when there is no child labour expended in fertilizing cotton seeds, or when the cotton is produced in an environmentally friendly fashion with the help of what is called Integrated Pest Management, it immediately makes other companies that are not thinking along these lines under tremendous pressure. It has an edge over them, and it has the added satisfaction of adding to knowledge.

Likewise, a firm can also insist that it will not buy parts from a producer that does not meet with the highest standards of compliance regarding working conditions, wages and benefits, and pollution standards. By being steadfast in this matter it can also raise the expectations of its consumers who will balk at the suggestion that some of what they consume has been produced under unacceptable conditions. Or, an enterprise may decide to purchase from co-operatives set up by marginal communities, or contract with service providers that come from backward sectors of the society. This also adds to the company's profile with its consumers, but again in a manner that affects the working of the organization in an intrinsic fashion.

These are some of the ways by which a company can have a sustainable CSR, and not be dependent on the mercurial dispositions of CEOs who themselves have ephemeral biographies within an organization. The mantra to sustainable CSR quite clearly is to relate it to principles of Business Ethics which forces one to reach out in terms of business interests within. Sustainable CSR is truly stakeholder oriented, and not just indiscriminate philanthropy.

Corporate Social Responsibility and Outreach

Business Ethics further requires a commitment to keep abreast of developments in knowledge and actually put them into operation. This aspect is as intimately linked to the issue of transparency as it is to the cause of advancing corporate social responsibility. Developments in knowledge take place both at the technological and at the human level. Safety regulations have become more stringent and exacting in many engineering and chemical companies simply because technological advances have shown up the dangers of earlier systems of production. Personnel relations, and interactions between levels and functions within companies, have also undergone changes in recent decades. Among other things it has been widely recognized that employee compliance comes more easily when initiatives and enterprise are adequately rewarded. In addition, market research and the growth of consumer lobbies have led to a greater degree of awareness of customer attitudes and responses. When an organization is alert on these fronts it is well on the way to being an ethical organization whether or not it donates sums of money for flood or famine relief.

An ethical concern can also advance corporate social responsibility by figuring out ways by which the world outside can be linked to its organizational functioning. If an enterprise's underwriting of worthy causes has no import on its functioning then Friedman is probably right in accusing executives of such an organization of going well beyond their brief. Business Ethics, however, aligns itself to larger social issues on a totally different plane in order to bring sustainability to CSR. The added advantage of this approach is that organizations are not woken up rudely after they face consumer anger, as it happened with Shell and Nike, but are prepared in advance. This prevents the possibility of unethical practice occurring in their business activities and CSR in this case can act as a protective instrument. There is yet another aspect to CSR that is often overlooked. I once asked a senior executive of IKEA what the company gained from their CSR activities. Without hesitating, he said, 'Greater professionalism within our organization.'

An ethical concern will figure out ways by which the world outside can be linked to its organizational functioning.

Though most companies active in this area are multinationals, it needs to be mentioned that their outreach efforts took place in India and in most cases they met with a large measure of success.

Can Indian companies learn from this? Indeed, the Tatas have been the traditional pacesetters in this regard. Their efforts for the advancement of the township of Jamshedpur are well-known. They introduced the eight hour working shift, 36 years before it became law in India, and prospered on account of it. Other enterprises should likewise think of how they can profitably integrate the logics and compulsions of their organizations with the needs of the broader society. When the corporate sector reaches out in this fashion its positive impact on society is much more lasting than old-fashioned philanthropy.

Good corporate citizenship does not emerge from the usual unidirectional philanthropic activities. In fact, many enterprises are turned off by this understanding of corporate social responsibility and thereby undermine it altogether. While everyone is welcome to be a philanthropist, it needs to be recognized that do-gooders are doing good on a highly personalized basis. If corporate social responsibility is identified principally with philanthropy then whenever there is a change of regime at the top, the philanthropic project either abruptly ceases, or changes direction, or becomes lifeless. In fact, the term corporate social responsibility is perhaps a little clumsy. Many IT professionals have pointed out to me that paying taxes and obeying the law are also aspects of corporate social responsibility—as indeed they are. Perhaps the term 'corporate outreach' is a more felicitous one. It best captures the spirit behind which executives strategize to relate themselves to the environment and community.

Why do corporate houses in India and even abroad prefer philanthropy to corporate outreach of the kind outlined above? I think this is primarily because corporate outreach demands a lot more careful and assiduous planning, which many of them find too arduous to commit themselves to.

In the ultimate analysis then it is through strict adherence to Business Ethics that the corporate sector can best promote social responsibility. There is little point in putting in a drop of charity when an ocean of goodwill is required. There is even less point in

There is little point in putting in a drop of charity when an ocean of goodwill is required.

donating to philanthropy and being absolutely unethical at home. Business Ethics not only adds to the organization's value, but also provides philanthropy with a sound doctrine and a reliable format within which it can maximize its contributions. Seen in this fashion, social responsibility of business is not really about charity. It is about positively impacting society in a manner that is good for business as well.

CHAPTER FIVE

FOR AN ETHICS GAME PLAN

Playing It Safe and Playing to Win

Business as Sport

Sport has often been likened to business, but we would do better if our businesses were run like sport. Remember professional sport is no leisure time activity. There are serious people out there who have dedicated their lives to a tough job that seems so easy from a distance. What separates fun and games from serious sport is the latter's dedication to win by the rules. As rules define the sport they must be open and in the domain of public knowledge. This enables the spectators, the consumers of sport, to enjoy a game well won.

Sport has often been likened to business, but we would do better if our businesses were run like sport.

The corporate world too plays to win. The point is: do they always play by the rules? In the closing years of the past century many sporting events like cricket, tennis and rugby were the preserve of gentlemen, aristocrats and pretenders, who perfected the art of losing gracefully. Over the years, the gradual formalization of rules encouraged the growth of professionalism in sport. This not only opened the door to the less privileged classes but also emphasized the need to win. Now that sport could be a source of livelihood and upward social mobility, many gentlemen found the heat hard to bear. Talent, more than birth or privilege, began to rule level playing fields.

Like sport, in business too, success depends on talent and enterprise and not on inherited advantages. But the analogy with sport need not stop here. The rules of sport are also very instructive for the corporate world. A closer look at these rules reveals that they are first and foremost about what *cannot* be done. Regardless of which sport we are talking about, there is just no compromise on what is prohibited. The challenge in a sporting event is how to score that goal, or make that run, without being penalized. Take away these rules and sport becomes a meaningless pantomime.

Leading by Example and Winning

Too often it is said: If my organization is ethical then it is bound to lose out when other organizations are free to lie, cheat and thieve as they please. It is like saying that good guys go to a very sanitized heaven, but the bad ones can go anywhere. Seen in this light ethics appears to be all cost and no investment. Obviously this is a serious enough allegation and must be attended to.

An organization that is run unethically can never stand up to first-rate competition anywhere in the world.

The fact that unethical organizations prosper needs to be checked out once more. As ethics begins first and foremost at one's workplace, an organization that is run unethically can never stand up to first-rate competition anywhere in the world. There will be too many chinks in one's armour and any smart competitor will lose no time in finding these out and taking full advantage of them. A good ethical organization is in fact a safe bet. You may not have instant success because you chose to go by ethical norms, but neither will you sink into oblivion overnight.

If the atmosphere in the workplace is unethical then it is impossible to combat the harsh vicissitudes of the outside world. Ethics consolidates office morale and boosts self-confidence among employees at all levels. Without a well-thought-out ethical compliance system one is taking a lot of risks. It then becomes difficult to predict how people in the organization will react to diverse temptations, tensions, and rivalries of the marketplace. Things may work out alright when times are good, but with the first crunch rats will leave the sinking ship with huge chunks of cheese.

True, the world is competitive and is made up of some of the meanest sharks that ever walked the earth. But if one has to be rough and tough with these folks then it is important that your flanks be covered. A strong ethical organization lets you take on the bad guys without constantly looking over your shoulder to make sure that your side is still intact. The home front must be secured first before making forays outside into the big, bad world. The world may be an evil place, but it would be very risky to venture into it with an uncoordinated side whose heart is not in the job but in a quick fix and a quick buck. Business Ethics tightens the home front into an effective fighting machine.

The home front must be secured before making forays outside into the big, bad world.

But as the old sporting adage goes: 'It is not winning or losing but how one plays the game that is important.' In the 1950s, when racial segregation was still prevalent in America, a little known school called Crispus Attucks in Illinois showed how a losing side can be the real victors.

Crispus Attucks was a segregated school for black children and was really quite ordinary by all counts. However, it managed to get a respectable basketball team that slowly improved with time. Soon the team became famous for its freewheeling style of play and began winning a few matches. Before long, it was hitting the headlines and raising expectations of all blacks in the neighbourhood.

Then one year the basketball team of Crispus Attucks just kept winning and winning. It eventually came to the finals in the school league. This upset many white basketball enthusiasts and put a lot of pressure on the long acknowledged leader in the field that came from an all-white school. The day before the final, the principal of Crispus Attucks told his basketball team that there was a lot of anger in the town on account of the fact that their school was doing so well. He warned his students that things might get rough in the finals but that they should always play by the rules. In the finals Crispus Attucks fought hard but lost. The other side had two extra players in the shape of the referees.

But the way Crispus Attucks played left an enormous impact. It strengthened the hands of those fighting racial segregation. It made white apologists think again. It gave the Black Civil Rights movement enormous fillip in the state of Illinois, particularly in the capital city of Indiana. Crispus Attucks went on perfecting their game and three years later they actually won the final. They raised their performance to such a level that even biased referees could not stop them.

Is there a lesson here for the corporate sector?

Practice, Practice, Practice

Ethics can sometimes seem very abstract and theoretical, something that is nice to think about when time permits but not on the priority list. But look closely: ethics is about what we do all the time whether we call it by that name or not.

Just as we don't imagine that an individual will grow from self-centred infancy to moral maturity without some guidance and discipline, we shouldn't assume that an organization of any size would be able to maintain its own integrity and responsibility without some explicit attention and maintenance. For that we need to practice, practice and practice.

Ethical practice, then, is not just 'right action', but is also an ongoing effort to develop and strengthen the habit of right action.

If the goal is ethical practice, then 'hiring good people' is only part of the job. One of the things managers can do in order to develop an organization where ethical practice is a matter of habit, is apply these two tests to policies and procedures at every level:

If the goal is ethical practice, then 'hiring good people' is only part of the job.

- Does the process make it easier for employees to understand and to implement the core values and principles (encourage right action)?
- Does the process make it more difficult to violate those values and principles (discourage misconduct)?

As more and more organizations work their way through developing, implementing, and evaluating ethics programmes, an approach that takes seriously both promotion and prevention is emerging as best practice. This should help good people to follow their good intentions in the complex and often contradictory environment of the modern workplace.

Own Up, Don't Cover Up

Every once in a while, quite naturally, because nobody's life is so well scripted in advance, one errs. Errors are part of the human condition. In fact, as the great sociologist Talcott Parsons argued, any theory that does not take into its ambit that human beings can err is woefully inadequate (Parsons 1959).

To err is human, but to cover up is wrong!

Our second mistake often is to cover up the first. It is this that makes us susceptible to unethical pressures from a variety of quarters. It is not as if all those who are now involved in some kind of unethical practice began their corporate lives with a strong desire to milk the system and profit at the organization's expense.

An easy admission of one's error usually slides away without leaving unpleasant memories.

What needs to be cultivated, deliberately, repeatedly and incessantly, is to quickly admit one's mistake before it gets too complicated. Far from the calamity some of us think that a confession might do to our careers, an easy admission of one's error usually slides away without leaving any unpleasant memories.

In fact, the ability to own up to one's errors arouses a fair amount of admiration from among those one feared would be the first to take advantage of the slip-up. Confessions of this sort purge the system of misperceptions and misapprehensions of one another. It also makes it that much harder for a bad egg to get away with wilful misdemeanour.

It is true that there is no tragedy, no matter how grim, from which someone is not drawing some satisfaction.

There will also be 'friends' who will be quite eager to help along in the cover-up. They now have you exactly where they want you to be. This is why an early admission of error takes away the fun from rumour-mongering and leaves professional detractors feeling rather stupid.

Adding on to the first mistake with a second, and so on, only compounds the first wrong move. At the end of the day the tally of things done wrong is far greater in number and gravity than the original error. Cover-ups, like corporate lunches, never come free. But lunches at least provide a momentary satisfaction that makes it easier to deliver later. A cover-up is distasteful from start to finish, and gets more and more distasteful with every subsequent coating.

The mistaken view that superiors are always ready to pounce on every error is what often leads to corrupt practices. The truth is, it is the capacity to own up to one's error that usually assures those at the top of a person's ability to discern and learn from one's mistakes.

The Bigger You Are the Harder the Fall

It was a fatal air crash that took Hansie Cronje away. Will people remember him as a great captain, or one who disgraced himself and the game of cricket by yielding to match-fixers?

In local-level tournaments, a transgression of a rule here and of a law there is of little significance. Nobody is watching that closely, and frankly, nobody really cares beyond the fun

When you are on the top, one wrong move can lead to serious credibility problems.

and the outing of the occasion. But in the big league the situation is very different. In this case everyone is watching. There is a whole crowd out there and they have invested serious time, energy, capital and commitment towards watching the progress of the game. This is why, when you are on top, one wrong move can lead to serious credibility problems.

Hansie Cronje was the idol of cricket lovers throughout the world, but he has left the world without being able to rehabilitate himself. A minor star could have got away with what Cronje had done, but not Cronje. This should be an object lesson to those companies that are today admired, revered, and even envied, by others in the corporate world. They should realize that their status at the top is assured as long as they can remain ethical.

Truly, the bigger you are the harder you fall!

As size matters, it is necessary for those who currently enjoy high levels of market respectability that they remain squeakily cleaner than those around them. Leading corporate organizations have to make doubly sure that transparency and integrity are not compromised at any level. It does not matter so much to them to lose a job or two, but they should not fudge with the basic norms of Business Ethics. A missed contract can always be overcome, but if the big players lose their credibility they can never surface again.

Business Ethics is a collective endeavour. Consequently it is incumbent on corporate leaders who appreciate the positive effects of Business Ethics to make sure that everyone in their teams is on the same wavelength on this matter, at least. Teamwork is effective when members not only realize that their individual strengths contribute to collective well-being, but also that an individual indiscretion can bring about their collective downfall.

Big boys had better be careful. They are being watched even at night.

When things go wrong in business, then executives react in one of two ways. They either follow the Tylenol model or the Firestone model. These models are very distinct from each other and, as we shall soon see, have very different implications for the company's bottom line. Both these models were leadership driven but with vastly different consequences.

Tylenol is a leading paracetamol and anti-pyretic drug in North America. It is used for coughs, colds, aches and pains, as well as for relieving pain after surgery. In 1982, a demented person tampered with Tylenol bottles and managed to insert cyanide tablets in many of them. This resulted in several deaths that were widely reported and covered by the press and mass media. Johnson & Johnson, the producers of Tylenol, immediately accepted responsibility for the incident and accordingly withdrew Tylenol of all strengths from every pharmaceutical shelf in North America. For months, Tylenol was not available for anyone anywhere. During this period, Johnson & Johnson went to work to produce an improved tamper-proof seal for Tylenol. When this seal was ready Tylenol was reintroduced in the market and it quickly reclaimed its position at the top.

Contrast this with what happened with Firestone Tires. Many incidents were reported where special utility vehicles (SUVs) equipped with Firestone tyres overturned on account of tyre bursts. This often resulted in the loss of life and, of course, grievous injuries. What did Firestone officials do? Top company executives initially denied that anything was wrong. Soon, they started putting the blame for these accidents at the door of the car manufacturer. This charge could not be sustained, as other makes that did not use Firestone tyres did not have such an accident-prone record. Then Firestone accused the drivers of SUVs of taking undue risks at very high speeds on extremely powerful machines. Firestone officials even found fault with newspaper reporters and portrayed them as ghoulish sensation-mongers.

However, these denials did not help. At the end of the day Firestone collapsed. Its dreadful track record (no pun intended) threw its employees out of work and put its stockholders in financial straits. Consequently, Firestone Tires went down in a heap of calumny and bad faith.

On the other hand, Tylenol is alive and very well. It is still helping millions of patients, providing jobs for workers, and earning shareholders healthy returns on their investments.

Transparency as a Credo

By owning up to one's errors, the hallowed cause of transparency takes on a very earthy and everyday connotation. There's much more to transparency than saying 'My ledger is an open book.' Facing one's errors head-on creates a genuine sense of camaraderie within the organization. It allows problems to be discussed in the open and accordingly, the solutions arrived at have a greater degree of social acceptance. By discussing one's errors, therefore, one is contributing to the advancement of knowledge. This is where transparency kicks in as a vital ethical marker.

Transparency is integral to an ethical enterprise because it uses knowledge to challenge itself to rise to greater heights. In this process it benefits itself as well as its stakeholders. Instead of hoarding knowledge in privileged quarters, corporate transparency treats knowledge as a currency of exchange.

As the Tylenol example shows, transparency is primarily about unabashedly embracing knowledge and rejoicing in its advances. If this were not the case then transparency would be a static concept, at best a passive demonstration of good faith. It would be no better than a tool that, once known, can be applied mechanically. As fresh challenges come up everyday, transparency must be operationalized in dynamic terms if it is to be meaningful. Just as potentialities for innovation are not exhausted by any single breakthrough, so also transparency cannot be limited to routine operations of tried and tested technologies. If the critical factor in innovation is to advance the boundaries of knowledge, then transparency is about extending the reach of this knowledge into further regions of corporate functioning.

Transparency is about embracing knowledge and rejoicing in its advances.

To be threatened by demands for greater knowledge and information is therefore incompatible with the foundational tenets of transparency. In the primitive days of early capitalism, knowledge was power and hence was sought to be concentrated and controlled. Such an attitude would be an anachronism today as customers and other stakeholders are much more assertive of their rights than they were in the past. Pressured in this fashion, transparency demands a buoyant and enquiring attitude towards knowledge.

There are several routine snares that trap transparency under the guise of efficiency and order. The most significant of them all goes under the name 'confidentiality'. Rarely do organizations review the criteria for confidentiality they may have inherited from an earlier dispensation. What may once have been considered confidential need not be so for all times to come. It is not as if confidentiality as a concept is out. Confidentiality in certain matters is necessary for a company to survive. In order to win an edge over an enterprise's real and potential competitors some knowledge advantage must exist. Nor can any organization allow insider trading without threatening its own existence. Such acts must be punished and severely discouraged. Trading information for selfish gain is totally different from advancing knowledge for greater stakeholder prosperity.

Even so, the criteria employed for bracketing away information as 'confidential' need to be constantly scrutinized and revised. This itself will release a lot of information and increase stakeholder participation. In a fiercely competitive atmosphere, enterprises need all the help they can get. Nothing can be more sustaining for a business organization than when its stakeholders enthusiastically rally around it.

The criteria for classifying information as 'confidential' need to be constantly reviewed.

As transparency is not a static concept, it is forced to evolve so that it can stay abreast of advances in the social environment. Knowledge expansion is an important aspect of such a dynamic setting, and an ethically transparent practice can ill afford to neglect this dimension.

It is not as if advancements in knowledge are always about scientific breakthroughs. Sometimes, they only advocate a change in perspective. Body Shop, for instance, is actively sponsoring research on the extent to which animal experiments are actually essential for laboratory sciences, and building support to ban such tests when not necessary.

Increments in knowledge take place at the so-called non-technological level as well. New accounting practices require a higher degree of information disclosure than what was earlier considered adequate. Rest assured that the drive for still greater transparency will lead to an even further refinement of such accounting procedures. Studies in human relations have demonstrated the tangible benefits of coupling monetary with moral remuneration.

If such advances in knowledge were not to be actively sought and put into actual practice, vital information and work skills would remain inaccessible to employees, customers, and shareholders. Entrepreneurial drive would slowly dry up at all levels, leading ultimately to organizational atrophy. Instead of initiatives welling up from below, it will be peeves and complaints. Corporate graveyards are full of companies that rested too long on their laurels. Such organizations inevitably turn opaque before they die.

Opaque Officialese

Every form of communication is an act of faith. This is certainly true of business writing when so much rides on being effective and practical. The writer must make every attempt to be clear, straightforward, and speak with an un-forked tongue.

Too often we fail to honour this faith—even when we don't intend to. Quick, sloppy, and unedited writing, as well as writing for effect, are prime sources of violations. It is not just bad writing but also bad ethics to say what we don't mean and fail to say what we do. The reader can become a defenceless victim of our lack of clarity. The crime is compounded when we use our writing to create impressions that are unwarranted.

It is not just bad writing but also bad ethics to say what we don't mean and fail to say what we do.

Few things are more depressing than writing to impress. Dressing up a report with irrelevant statistics and facts just because they look good, wastes the reader's time and gives out the wrong messages all too often. To quote sources that are either redundant or besides the point can again be misleading to the unsuspecting reader.

Writing makes the best impression when it is crafted in as unambiguous a way as possible. When no concessions are made to hyperbole and superfluities, the reader feels immediately rewarded. The instructions are clear, the facts are laid out face forward, and the conclusions drawn come through logically and without fuss. To obfuscate and doublespeak can only appeal to those who are given to superficial impression management.

Honest writing honours the reader. This is why writing clearly is to write ethically. Business writing, which includes corporate reports, summaries, training manuals, project proposals, should honour the readers and not breach the act of faith with which the reader goes through the written word. Very simply this means a commitment to communicate as clearly as possible, and to the best of one's ability.

If time is money then a wrong reading is a waste in every sense of the *word.*

When Rules Enable

There is another kind of opacity that blind officiousness encourages. How often has a good initiative been stumped by the admonition: 'That's against the rules.' Almost everyone, at some stage in one's career, has been frustrated by the inflexibility of rules. This is why it is important to remember what rules are meant to do and what they are not meant to do.

Rules should not be seen as strictures that prohibit but rather as enabling mechanisms. A rule should ideally be read as a way of doing things effectively: to get the best out of the team. Consequently, the course of action that a rule prohibits is because it would promote inefficiency within, and harm to, the organization. This is why rules should be thoroughly reasoned out before they are framed and put to work. Very often certain rules are just handovers from the past that nobody has really bothered to question. The longevity of these rules is less because of their efficacy and more on account of sheer office inertia.

Rules should not be seen as strictures that prohibit but rather as enabling mechanisms.

Once rules are in place they should not be trifled with. Whimsically bending rules is probably the worst thing one could do for office discipline. Yet so often the temptation to do exactly this is very strong. This is especially so when the original intention behind a rule is lost and the rule now looms as a prohibitive clause and nothing more. A good rule at one point in time may become a drag and a hindrance at a later date. After all, the world around us is changing all the time. This makes some rules redundant and, by the same token, requires other rules to be placed on the anvil.

This is why it is important to periodically review the book of rules no matter how obedient the office staff has been on the whole. Enterprises are usually very sensitive to customer feedback and attend to it very assiduously in the hope of maximizing customer satisfaction. Yet many of these enterprises do not apply the same standards when it comes to internal office management. For the staff there are rules which are engraved in stone, but for the outside world there is all the compassion, understanding and goodwill.

This kind of duality is not helpful for the overall functioning of the firm. Once the rationale behind rules is clear then compliance to them is easily won. As a result there is greater commitment to the workplace and much larger portions of energy in interactions with customers and clients.

Making Exceptions According to Rules

While every organization must frame rules that apply to all, there are times when exceptions have to be made. In this connection it is worth asking whether there is an ethical way of making exceptions to the rule?

Indeed there is!

First, while making the rule, care should be taken that the rule is neither unrealistic nor blatantly unfair. It should not, without adequate justification, lack uniformity in application. Very often there is an unseeming haste in fashioning a rule without taking into consideration certain ground realities. But once a rule is made it should be adhered to, and that should be the aim of all rule-makers. They should think of all kinds of possible objections to a rule before it is formulated, but after it is put down, it has to be strictly observed in letter and spirit.

Alongside, it is equally important to devise as to how exceptions to the rule will be handled, should the occasion for doing so come up. Such rules need to be made well in advance—well before the actual need to make an exception arises.

Rules for making exceptions should be based on the following guidelines:

1. Seeking exception must not be made easy. Sanction must be sought at a very high level. Taking the matter to such senior levels will itself be an inhibiting factor in seeking exceptions. The further advantage is that when all relevant decision-makers concur *Seeking exception to a rule must not be made easy.* to a very specific exception to a certain rule, then that furthers the norm of transparency.

2. On no account should exceptions to the rule break the law of the land.

3. Finally, no exceptions to the rule should tamper with the company's code of conduct.

By making room for exceptions to the rule in this manner, it is possible to meet the twin objectives of uniformity and fairness.

Uniformity versus Fairness

In keeping with the increasing emphasis on transparency, the corporate sector in recent years has taken the matter of setting up rules and regulations very seriously. From my own experience, I find that the workforce is happier in institutions that observe, without exception, clearly stated rules. The level of discontent is much higher in those organizations where almost everything is negotiable.

Having said this it is also necessary to emphasize that uniformity of rules should be based on ethical foundations that have a broadbased acceptability within the organization. All too often one hears the complaint in enterprises that have firm rules and guide-

Rules must not only be uniform but also fair.

lines that there is no heart and feeling in the work atmosphere. For example, sick leave rules may be unfair to a person whose illness is unusually grave. Or travel expenses often cannot take into account problems encountered on an especially difficult terrain. Such instances can be multiplied. When this is brought to the notice of the top management they feel extremely disappointed. They worked very hard to craft a set of rules and business policies that apply to all without exception in order to be unprejudiced, and now they are told that they are not being fair. If it is not one thing it is the other! So how can the issue of fairness be addressed adequately so that the legitimacy behind uniformity of rules is not undermined?

This indeed is a tough call. There are no easy answers, but perhaps the following considerations, if kept in mind, might provide some solutions.

i) Make sure that the rules do not seem to be entirely top-driven. Very often there is a covert, and unrecognized, hostility at not being consulted before decisions are taken.

ii) There should be references in the body of rules to other rules that allow for exceptional circumstances. These exceptional circumstances should be listed out as exhaustively as possible along with the level of authority at which such exceptions can be granted. In this case it is indeed extremely necessary to understand the actual dilemmas that confront management in their day-to-day activities. This again demands interactive sessions and workshops.

iii) Make sure there isn't that single ridiculous rule that spoils it all. Sometimes in the zeal to be foolproof certain rules are framed that give the impression that the top management either thinks very poorly of the intellectual level of those below them, or suspects them of every conceivable impropriety.

iv) There should be routine reviews of these rules at regular intervals.

v) Finally, and most importantly, deliberate and self-conscious attempts must be made to relate these rules to ethical norms (see The Importance of Synergy, Chapter 2). This is the surest way to get a buy-in from management at all levels on an enduring basis.

Conflicts and Interests

Balancing and resolving conflicting interests is an essential task of management. But not every conflict between interests constitutes a 'conflict of interest'.

A conflict of interest exists when someone is required to exercise independent judgement or to give objective advice, but stands to personally gain or lose from any of the options being considered. Independence and objectivity may be called into question when the chance to advance self-interest is present.

The existence of a conflict of interest is neither good nor bad in itself. Whether it poses a problem depends upon a number of circumstances such as materiality, the level of independence required and disclosure.

When a conflict of interest is disclosed and the potential gain or loss is below any reasonable threshold of materiality, the parties concerned may decide to ignore the conflict. Further, when a conflict of interest is disclosed, the parties concerned may decide that the personal integrity of the one with the conflict is an adequate assurance of objectivity. In cases where the highest level of independence is required, even the appearance of a conflict of interest is unacceptable and the one with the conflict must be excluded from the decision.

Failure to disclose a conflict of interest is a recipe for ethical disaster.

The key to dealing with conflict of interest is disclosure. Disclosure promotes transparency, and transparency is one of the principal building blocks of trust. Disclosure of all conflicts of interest needs to be a matter both of policy and of practice. Clear guidelines and reliable advice should be readily available when questions of conflict arise.

Simply *having* a conflict of interest may not be a major problem, but *failure to disclose* a conflict of interest is a recipe for ethical disaster.

Three Ways Out of Trivia

In ancient Rome a three-way crossroads was known as 'trivia'—literally, *tri-via*, or three routes. On such important junctions signboards were put up indicating the way to different parts of the country. Not all arrows in such places pointed to Rome, only one did. But the signs to major destinations had little appendages dangling from them indicating the lesser towns and villages en route. These crossroads, or trivia, also turned out to be natural places to carve graffiti saying all manner of rude and improper things. Over time the directions to big cities were crowded out by a mass of unimportant details. This is how the term trivia gained its current meaning.

Trivia therefore has a way of pushing important things into the background. What might seem quite harmless at first sight need not necessarily be quite as innocuous on closer scrutiny. Top executives have to constantly decide in the daily round of their activities as to what is trivial and what is not. Quite true to form, there are three ways of handling the trivia as well.

One option is to consider all trivial things as being too inconsequential to take note of. If there is some

There are three ways out of trivia. Which route would you take?

fudging in the expense account but it does not amount to much, why waste time over it? If an employee takes an economy class ride and claims business class, it is a small matter as the person was entitled to business class anyway. No need to fuss; let it go!

The other way of handling trivial matters is to insist that every issue, no matter how insignificant it may appear, be brought to the superior for sanction and approval. So long as the boss knows about it, all is well. It is then up to the discretion of those at the top to designate a certain thing as trivial and some other things as grave.

The third way out is to make it abundantly clear within the company as to what is trivial and what is not. Once this is agreed upon it should apply to all without fear or favour. In order to impress this uniformity across the board it is the responsibility of the top management to lead by example. To firm up this position it is important to hold regular drills and workshops that emphasize how important it is not to do the wrong thing no matter how small it may appear. It can be easily demonstrated that a tiny step in the wrong direction leads to much larger problems down the road.

So there are three ways out of trivia. Not all roads, in this case, lead to Rome. Which route would you take?

CHAPTER SIX

IN TIMES OF TROUBLE

Recognizing Red Flags

It's Not Easy

When President Kennedy was questioned about America's space programme, he said: 'We don't do things because they are easy, we do them because they are tough.'

Business Ethics too is tough. Making sure your business runs ethically is far from being easy. The toughest part is to be able to say 'No'. This can make you unpopular with friends, relations and with the old boy network.

It is true that all organizations operate on a good deal of informality. Over time this tends to bond into a camaraderie that is often beneficial to the company. Too often, however, this camaraderie evolves from an unwritten pact that values friendship above company values. This is what allows ethical malpractice to go by undetected till it is too late.

To be able to set aside networks of friendship in the conduct of business practice is not always a popular thing to do. People have to pay a price for this. But those who cannot overcome the old boy network have to pay a much higher price in the long run.

Those who cannot overcome the old boy network have to pay a high price in the long run.

We are all susceptible to being pressured against our better judgement. When friendships are involved emotions tend to get the upper hand. After all how can one tell on a friend! But as a friend, it is also our duty to keep our friendship on an even keel.

Sometimes a small favour out of turn can become the beginning of a mutual non-aggression pact between colleagues. 'You don't tell on my little indiscretions on the side, and I won't tell on what you are up to.' The hard part about being ethical is the constant pressure to put yourself, and those around you, under constant scrutiny. Only the tough survive such continuous monitoring.

It is the weak who break down. Unfortunately, when they do so they do not go down alone. In contemporary businesses the reputation of one is linked to the reputation of all. In recent times some of the highest-powered corporate executives were caught red-handed with their hands in the till. Unfortunately, their disgrace damaged others who were employed by the same firm. This is why, in the corporate world today, setting in place Business Ethics procedures can protect those who are innocent. Once an organization ratifies a full-fledged Business Ethics system it not only means a continuous drill regarding what is unacceptable, that is, a code of conduct, but it will also help managers and executives at all levels spot red flags when they pop up. These are of extreme relevance in times of trouble. For red flags to be noticed and properly addressed, it is necessary to have a grievance mechanism in place where complaints, fears and apprehensions can be registered.

A Wailing Wall

According to folk wisdom, a good cry often lightens a heavy heart. It is surprising how performance levels go up once we get things off our chest. It is important then that the corporate sector too institutionalizes ways of handling frustrations and complaints before they get out of hand, become ugly, and tell on the organization's performance. But according to the 1999 KPMG Business Ethics survey in India, only 39 per cent of the respondents said that their companies had a grievance cell. Even fewer—only 14 per cent—said that they had an ombudsman's office in place.

Many conflict situations, whether domestic, corporate or international, are based on misperceptions of one another and not on hard facts. After the damage is done the overwhelming question usually is: 'Was it worth it, after all?' It is only when we survey the destruction do we realize that the waste could have been avoided had we just taken time off to frankly talk about our problems. In which case none of the devastation need have happened at all.

Pet peeves have a way of growing into unmanageable monsters. It is best therefore to tackle them at birth and not give them room to spread and multiply. A grievance cell, or an ombudsman's office, if handled sensitively, helps to make for a happier workforce. To be able to cry at the right place and to get a sympathetic ear dramatically reduces the burden of sorrow. As most of the grievances reported are fed largely on misperceptions, they are not difficult to resolve. In fact, they can be sorted out quite painlessly.

A grievance cell, or an ombudsman's office, helps to make for a happier workforce.

While the direct benefit of this is, of course, a greater degree of commitment to the job, management can also get interesting insights from a grievance cell. Such a cell should not be seen simply as a safety valve mechanism, but as a vital source for learning as well. Management correctives can be significantly informed by the kinds of grievances that come up from all quarters.

No Excuses for Bad Apples

According to the 2002 KPMG forensic survey in India, over 70 per cent of frauds came to light because they were reported by stakeholders, from employees to distributors. Obviously, it pays to have a grievance cell, an ombudsman, a wailing wall, where complaints can be registered, and where the complainant knows that the investigation will be impartial.

According to the 1999 KPMG Business Ethics survey in India, the greatest ethical risk to the corporate sector was perceived to be the misuse of confidential information. As many as *71 per cent* of respondents felt that this was the single greatest source of unethical practice in business organizations. Interestingly, the Canadian KPMG Business Ethics survey came up with very similar conclusions with respect to Canada.

The greatest ethical risk to the corporate sector is perceived to be the misuse of confidential information.

If the perception that confidential information may be misused is so high then there are probably good reasons for it. In addition, knowledge assets and intellectual property are today in the form of electronic data that can be moved and even deleted with a feather touch on a button.

It is necessary to take pre-emptive steps against leaks in, and misuse of, confidential information as well as to be firm with those who have abused the trust of the organization. It is also worthwhile reinforcing that certain acts, like insider trading, are criminal offences and that no quarter will be given to those who are guilty of such conduct within the company.

On occasions it is necessary to *make an example* of those who have indeed betrayed the trust of the organization. In this connection it should be kept in mind that the extent of the actual damage at any one instance may not be very extensive but the potential loss and harm arising from the misuse of confidential information cannot be underestimated. Tardiness in responding to known acts of information betrayal and misuse will only send out the wrong kind of message.

Effective management must increasingly depend upon commitment and trust. Command and control are not always feasible. But when hard decisions have to be taken, any equivocation will obviously be out of place. An attitude of trust can have positive consequences if built on a conscientiously applied programme of transparency and regular accountability. This would help strike the necessary balance between cynical suspicion and naïve confidence.

Despite efforts to manage the ethics process, there will always be individuals intent on doing the wrong thing. How can you spot potential problems and take corrective action?

Red Flags

KPMG's Business Ethics and integrity practice has identified a number of specific 'red flags' that may point to potential problems:

- **Lifestyle**

An affluent lifestyle that is not consistent with employment earnings may be supported by family wealth or an inheritance, or it may be funded by fraud.

- **Vacations**

An employee who never takes a vacation may just love the job, but reluctance to let go of the controls may also indicate an effort to hide misconduct.

- **Tolerance to Small Liberties**

A pattern of taking liberties with policy and procedures may be given the gloss of 'flexibility', but this may also provide a smoke screen for misconduct.

- **High Employee Turnover**

When too many people leave a department, or express an interest to leave a department, then that is cause for concern.

- **Unclear Annual Reports**

When the annual report gives the impression of being too slick, watch out!

When reports, including annual reports, are written in an unclear fashion, with far too much technical jargon, unnecessary charts and figures—in short, when it gives the impression of being too slick, watch out!

It is important to investigate such red flags and, where required, take appropriate action. Employees who see others profiting from misconduct can become cynical about the value of ethical practice. Quite apart from the benefit of preventing a particular loss, investigations of questionable behaviour can help communicate a commitment to ethical practice. An effective investigation can also help to determine whether the problem is, in fact, related to an individual or is a symptom of a weakness in the ethical structure of the organization.

Upward communication channels, education and training for ethical awareness, a code of conduct, and a transparent decision-making process contribute to an ethical culture where the *right* thing is the *done* thing. An added benefit of such a culture is that individuals intent on misconduct find that they tend to stand out as exceptions and will either change their ways or find a more tolerant work environment elsewhere.

Exposure of unethical conduct is usually followed by one or more standard excuses:

> 'I didn't know it was wrong.'
>
> 'Everyone else does it.'
>
> 'I didn't think it would hurt anyone.'
>
> 'It was the only way to get the job done.'

The excuse we almost never hear (even though it is applicable 90 per cent of the time) is, 'I thought I could get away with it.'

Many companies have a clearly stated policy against taking bribes. Many companies go a step further and also prohibit, in no uncertain terms, the giving of bribes. In fact, several multinationals are forbidden by law in their home countries against offering bribes in any of their operations anywhere in the world. If found guilty of this charge these companies would face severe sanctions at home, if not in the arena where the illegal transaction actually took place.

While there is some clarity regarding taking and receiving bribes, most companies are very unsure about how they should handle the person who tries to bribe their officials. Usually, if a company is self-consciously ethical—the employees of the firm would refuse a bribe when offered. This, however, is not sufficient. If organizations are serious about their anti-bribery stance they should take the matter further and penalize the briber as well.

If the bribe is merely rejected then the briber faces no risks whatsoever. A chance was taken, it did not work out, and that is the end to it. Obviously, the briber is getting the best of both worlds. If the bribe is accepted, the job is done, and if it is not, well, nothing is lost.

The only way to seal off such situations is to penalize the bribers by taking the company's work and custom away from them. Thus, if the company's travel agent, or dealer, or supplier, has offered a bribe, the reaction should be to reject the bribe, of course, but in addition, to blacklist this person in the company's record.

It is not enough to reject bribes; the briber must be penalized.

If such penalties are not imposed then it leaves the briber free to chance the arm repeatedly in the hope that some time in the future defences will crumble and the job will get done. This is why the best way to deal with such a situation is to immediately notify one's superior that a bribe was offered and make sure that the briber is shown the door as far as future work with the company is concerned.

One important role of a corporate ethics or compliance programme is to take away all the excuses. Without excuses, responsibility sits squarely on the shoulders of the decision-maker. Without excuses, temptation is much less attractive.

By clarifying and communicating the values, code of conduct, principles and standards of the organization, and supporting these explicit statements with ongoing training and education, ignorance of the law is no longer a valid excuse. Monitoring, auditing and internal reporting heighten the awareness of ethics and compliance issues and their impact on the organization. Effective oversight also makes 'getting away with it' much harder to imagine.

Impartial enforcement of the rules and application of explicit consequences take care of the myth that 'everyone does it'. Winking at misconduct when the rules are unambiguous only encourages excuses that lead to serious damage. The most potent element of an effective ethics or compliance programme is senior management's rock solid commitment to lead by example in an organization where the law is respected and upheld, where the truth is told and promises are kept, where hard decisions are made with courage and justice, and where integrity is the key to success. It is also under these circumstances that a full-fledged grievance mechanism can be expected to work effectively and impartially.

No excuses!

The moment one begins to make excuses, something dreadful happens, and so many get hurt. This is exactly what happened in the infamous Enron case.

Handcuff Accessories for Enron Bosses

They have not come up yet with designer handcuffs that go with business suits. After the indictment of very senior executives of Enron, WorldCom, Arthur Andersen, and so on, it might be a good idea to market handcuffs as accessories for the rich and infamous. In days to come corporate kings would not like to be captured by TV cameras in ill-fitting and noncoordinated handcuffs.

But is all this excitement another example of American exceptionalism with little impact on the corporate world elsewhere? Or are there lessons here that we would do well to heed in India? It is true that George Bush was stung to the quick by what happened with Enron and Arthur Andersen and he passed the tough Sarbanes-Oxley Act. Henceforth a chief executive officer would be held responsible if the company fudged accounts, cooked its ledger books, or, in short, misled shareholders and the public. The sentence for such an offence is a punitive twenty years in prison. If punishment is based on the theory of deterrence then this should probably work in combating such starched white-collar crimes.

Can the American public and shareholders now relax? The deterrence theory of jurisprudence has some serious critics who argue that there will always be criminal minds at work thinking of the latest way of breaking the law. How then can ordinary people—the taxpayers, the small shareholder—get any protection if the law can always be bent and broken by a new generation of corporate fraudsters. This is an important question in America as almost 25 per cent of Americans today hold shares in different companies. No wonder the public there is so concerned and incensed at how the corporate sector has discredited itself.

The lesson from big time corporate frauds is that rather than trust anybody you should use your own judgement.

The lesson from the latest big time corporate frauds is that rather than trust anybody you should use your own judgement. If a reputed auditing company like Arthur

Andersen can be implicated in the Enron scandal (and a few others besides) then who can the ordinary share-holder turn to for authentic information? It is also common knowledge now that annual reports of even reputed companies can be very misleading. The bottom line can be made to look good or bad, depending on what the senior executives want it to be. Profits are hyped if companies want to boost their market shares and thereby enhance their credit ratings. Profits can be lowered in the books if the enterprise wants to duck paying taxes. Ordinary shareholders and members of the taxpaying public are very often left holding the can even after they had very assiduously perused the annual reports and balance sheets of companies.

The scandals in Enron, WorldCom and Xerox have hurt India as well though not as hard. But as more and more Indians get drawn into the shares game they had better watch out. By and large Indian shareholders are very forgiving. They continue to hold on to stocks even though they underperform dreadfully year after year. There are indications, however, that this might soon change. Companies are aggressively advertising them-selves against projected profits in the hope of winning over prospective investors. There have been some signal disaster stories in this respect, but even so there are many who get carried away by these promises. After all, most of us do not have the technical knowledge to understand what is being said in financial statements. Even when we have some expertise in this regard we are not sure to what extent the credit ratings are to be trusted. Enron has stated in its defence that it did indeed disclose information about related-party transactions, but as all that was made in very cryptic footnotes nobody really got a hang of what was being said. So on the face of it, Enron abided by the letter of the law set by the

Financial Accounting Standards Board, even while they successfully violated every bit of it in spirit.

Very often employees of these companies are in the know of what is going on but they are so seduced by employee stock option plans that they become willing partners in corporate frauds. There is a general acquiescence from top down to dupe the ordinary shareholder. Margaret Ceconi, who was once the director of sales in Enron Energy Services, sent e-mails all the way up in her company pointing out that something was very seriously wrong in the way profits were being posted. Profits were booked even before services were delivered and calculated on the basis of aggressive estimates of what energy prices were going to be in the future. According to Ceconi, she smelt a rat soon after she joined the organization and it was not as if she was alone. It was common knowledge among her colleagues, and a bit of a joke as well, that the books were being cooked on a massive scale and that all of this was in their interests because they held stocks in their own company.

Often employees get so seduced by stock option plans that they become willing partners in corporate frauds.

So no matter how closely we read financial statements of companies it is impossible to know exactly what is going on. After all, Enron was the darling of Wall Street's many financial analysts and wizards. Nor can we always depend on the laws to protect us from corporate frauds. When there is big money involved there are always interested political parties that are also in the act, providing good protective shields for buccaneer entrepreneurs. Don't forget that President George W. Bush affectionately called Kenneth Lay, the now errant chief of Enron, 'Kenny boy' in the pre-bust-up days. An Enron consultant was a White House economic adviser, an Enron vice-president became secretary of the army, and Harvey Pitt, the lawyer who argued for Arthur Andersen, was appointed by President Bush to head the Securities and Exchange Commission.

The only way citizens everywhere can protect themselves is to be able to read red flags when they pop up, regardless of what financial analysts and credit rating agencies may say. The first thing to watch out for is when share prices shoot up phenomenally. It could be an index of genuine growth as with some infotech stocks, but in some cases it may be a spurious spurt. So it is worth checking out. Enron shares jumped to as high as US$ 90 before the crash.

The only way citizens can protect themselves from corporate frauds is to be able to read red flags when they pop up.

The second red flag is when the annual report is couched in plenty of jargon and is largely incomprehensible. Unreadable statements of this kind usually conceal something quite dark and sinister. This is one of the oldest subterfuges in the world. The third red flag is when the big guns in the company are very cosy with the powers that be. In such cases the temptation to break the law and depend on political patronage is very strong. Sooner or later pay time will come and it will be the poor stockholder and employees of the organization who will lose out the most. Finally, be a little careful of organizations where the employee stock option is factored in as part of salary remuneration. In this case it is very tempting for everyone in the organization to keep share prices up in the stock exchange even when real business is going down the tube.

Some of us may get some malicious pleasure in seeing handcuffs on business suits. But for so many it is really tragic as life's savings are lost because of corporate greed. This is why it is necessary for the ordinary person to start taking control directly over how and where his money is being invested. We can no longer trust balance sheets, stock prices, and financial analysts. What we need to do is to watch out for warning signals and take corrective action. This will force companies to behave, and the crooked ones to fold up. This is how democracy can be made to work in the corporate sector.

Alarm bells are already ringing in India. The non-performing assets (NPAs) in the banking sector in this country stood at Rs 805.74 billion in March 2001. This has recently begun to draw some attention and scrutiny. We now also know that the biggest defaulters in paying up loans to the banks are major figures in the Indian corporate sector. The list of such people reads like the 'who's who' of the Indian business elite. One business house alone accounts for roughly 10 per cent of the NPAs of the banking sector. It is argued that if these companies are getting away with it they must have enormous political influence. But sooner or later somebody will have to pay. Must it always be the common person?

Small Beginnings for Big Frauds

We tend to take our eyes off the ball because all too often big frauds have small beginnings. Only much later they work up to a respectable scam. Recently, the world saw a vivid drama on television sponsored by Tehelka.com when some Indian politicians and their cohorts were filmed taking bribes. The initial amounts were not much, but a whole lot was promised. This is where there is a similarity between the Tehelka.com revelations and the 2001 KPMG fraud survey conducted in India.

KPMG ethics audits in India over the years show that though frauds drain companies of millions of rupees, a lot of this happens in very small doses through the padding of expense accounts. Respondents to the 2001 KPMG fraud survey believe that about 35 per cent of rupee losses due to fraud take place because of inflated expense accounts.

A KPMG survey in India found that about 35 per cent of rupee losses due to fraud take place because of inflated expense accounts.

While such frauds may not involve huge sums of money at one go, and hence often remain undetected, the company is slowly bled over a long period of time with no end in sight. The KPMG ethics audits reveal that, if totalled, they would add up to a staggering sum.

Sadly, companies wake up to expense account-related fraud only when some gross discrepancies are detected, that is, well after the damage has been done. Damage control is clearly not enough in such cases. The management must also think seriously of how to prevent such frauds from taking place in the first instance. For every fraud detected there is a lot more that simply goes unnoticed. This daily dribbling, sapping of a firm's finances needs to be addressed. This cannot be done solely through internal audit reviews.

Often, it's the small things that act as red flags. It may not just be about the doctoring of expense accounts. Secret commissions and insider trading could be going on as well. Even if it is merely the tip that has been exposed, it should alert the top management to thinking seriously about the stated and unstated aspects of the company's culture. It is the unstated parts that often create problems.

When expense accounts are being fraudulently inflated on a fairly large scale, it is incumbent upon the senior management to enquire as to how their employees got the wrong signals. If the employees feel that padding expense accounts is such a minor indiscretion that it is almost acceptable, then that impression needs to be corrected.

Second, as the 2001 KPMG fraud survey reveals, though internal audit reviews and controls play a large part in detecting fraud, it is equally important to win the trust of employees, dealers and customers if frauds are to be contained. These other stakeholders of the company should feel motivated and confident enough to register their complaints with senior management whenever they notice any fraudulent activity within the organization. If roughly 72 per cent (according to KPMG) of frauds are brought to light by stakeholders, then it is necessary that attention be given to oiling this aspect of the company's machinery so that those who come to know of fraudulent activities will not hesitate to report them. Obviously, this implies that top management must be able to project that they are serious about these complaints and that these would be investigated no matter who is implicated and regardless of where the complaint comes from.

This strategy would also bring about a lower tolerance threshold level amongst all those who have a stake in the company, primarily the employees. Top management must be sensitive to the fact that it needs allies at various levels within the organization as well as outside it. This is not only an effective and cost-free strategy for curbing fraud, but is also a tried and tested way of eliminating the damaging distinction that often arises between 'us' and 'them' within the firm and outside it.

The Ethics of Whistle-Blowing

One can now also add to our list of red flags, organizations that do not respect the ethics of whistle-blowing. If whistle-blowing had been encouraged, then Enron would not have damaged the lives of so many innocent employees and stockholders around the globe.

According to the *Economist* Intelligence Unit Online Survey (July 2002), as many as 51 per cent of the respondents believe that cultural and managerial hostility to whistle-blowing is one of the principal barriers to the implementation of corporate governance. This hostility to whistle-blowing is indeed disturbing.

Managerial hostility to whistle-blowing is a barrier to corporate governance.

There are some lessons we learn at school that are often difficult to unlearn later in life. In the schoolyard code of ethics you never tell on a fellow student. No matter how gross or snooty the offending person might be, mum's the word especially where school authorities are concerned. Those who break this rule are jeered at by other students. They are called tattle-tales, squealers, boobies, and rats. And these, mind you, are only the more printable terms of abuse that are hurled at them.

What might seem honourable in those relatively innocent schoolgoing days need not always be so, especially when we enter the adult world of business and corporate activity. A prank, a practical joke, an occasional bout of foul play in school is not as damaging as adult white-collar crime can be. According to the above-mentioned KPMG fraud survey, at least Rs 5 billion was lost over the past five years on account of corporate fraud. This is only the tip of the iceberg; the actual damage is definitely much greater.

Very often it is believed that whistle-blowers are dissatisfied, frustrated cranks, and not well-wishers of the company. Yet, the motive behind such whistle-blowing is rarely personal aggrandizement. In most instances, whistle-blowers prefer to remain anonymous precisely because of this pervasive negative attitude towards them.

There are several ways of generating a healthy culture of whistle-blowing. To begin with, it is a good idea for all major organizations to institute the office of an ombudsman who will impartially go into all complaints and make sure that due process is observed in addressing these grievances.

It is also worthwhile to have an ethics hotline where complaints can be registered, even by anonymous callers. Perhaps if this hotline were manned by an outside agency it might help create an atmosphere of fairness. This would certainly reduce the sense of fear that haunts whistle-blowers. In fact, come to think of it, whistle-blowing happens far too rarely given the extent of white-collar crime in this country and elsewhere.

Whistle-blowing happens far too rarely given the extent of white-collar crime in India.

In our experience, most companies do not like to entertain anonymous complaints. This seems fair enough because crank calls and letters venting petty jealousies might snarl the whole process. In many organizations there could be a flood of complaints around promotion time against potential competitors. When individual rivalry rather than company welfare spurs such activities, anonymous whistle-blowing can be a regular source of nuisance.

On the other hand, if organizations insist that those who file complaints clearly identify themselves, then the whistle-blowers might balk at the prospect of going out on a limb to tell against a colleague. There would be a great degree of reluctance in sticking one's neck out, particularly if the systems of enquiry and investigation have not been formalized, nor gained a degree of acceptability, within the organization.

It is difficult to make a blanket recommendation on which form of whistle-blowing should be entertained — the anonymous or the non-anonymous. In some companies anonymous complaints have worked, in others not quite as well. In my knowledge there is at least one case where the number of anonymous whistle-blowers decreased with the management's ability to demonstrate, over a period of time, its sincerity in investigating complaints.

For whistle-blowing to have a positive effect on the organization concerned, three minimal conditions have to be met:

(1) Investigating every complaint.

(2) Not fearing crank calls.

(3) Setting up an ombudsman's office.

1. *Investigating every complaint.* If whistle-blowers are to be encouraged then they should be reassured

against retribution. In order to do so, it must be demonstrated that every complaint will be investigated as transparently and fairly as possible. Regardless of whom the complaint is against, if the person is found guilty then sanctions and punishment must follow.

2. *Protect the confidentiality of the whistle-blower.* The whistle-blower must be protected against harassment and undue pressure. This can be best done by respecting the confidentiality of the complainant even if the charge be later proved to be false. In any case no action should be taken without prima facie evidence against the accused.

3. *Companies should not fear crank calls.* In the name of cutting out crank calls, many companies refuse to entertain anonymous complaints. If whistle-blowing is respected as a reliable way of catching frauds in time, then all complaints should be looked into. Once credibility is established within the organization with respect to meting out justice, truly and fairly, the number of anonymous complaints goes down. More and more whistle-blowers are emboldened to put down their names.

4. *Make known the procedures.* The whistle-blower should be told of the time frame and the procedure for investigating the charge.

5. *The ombudsman must enjoy high credibility.* There has to be someone to whom whistle-blowers can go. For whistle-blowing to be effective, it has to be institutionalized. There should be a systematic way by which complaints get heard and registered. Most importantly, in this connection, the

person in charge should be someone who enjoys enormous credibility within the company for fair play as well as for competence. This person would be performing the role of an ombudsman regardless of what the actual designation may be. In case there is a lack of unanimity on who this person should be, or if the designated official is already overladen with responsibilities, then perhaps a specialized consulting agency could be considered to filter, enquire, and process complaints. One way or another, every company should have institutionalized ways of entertaining whistle-blowers.

It all boils down then to a question of generating trust within the organization. If there is a well-thought-out policy on whistle-blowers a company can save itself financial and moral damage of a very high order. It needs also to be recognized in this process that a schoolboy tattletale has little in common with adult whistle-blowing. The risks are truly enormous and cannot be ignored except at one's peril. There is only one way of countering unethical practices and that is by making it difficult for those within the organization to indulge in them. 'Take care of the inside and the outside will take care of itself' should be the *mantra* for our times.

The Leopard Skin Chief

What are the qualities you should look for when choosing an ombudsman for your organization?

The role of an ombudsman is increasingly being appreciated in modern corporate offices. He is supposed to listen to complaints in the strictest of confidence, sift misunderstandings from serious misdemeanours, and seek solutions to grievances in a transparent, rule-abiding fashion.

It is for this reason that ombudsmen are so essential for the maintenance of high ethical standards within an organization. By performing these tasks an ombudsman keeps communication channels open. This prevents pet peeves from growing into gigantic grouses, protects whistle-blowers, and consequently helps nip potential wrongdoing in the bud.

This is all very well, but who is to be the ombudsman? Many companies employ a person specifically for this purpose. Some others hire outside help. They come in at periodic intervals, do their job, clean up their desks, and leave. The best option, however, is when someone from within the company is given this responsibility.

The person chosen as ombudsman should have a sterling, almost charismatic, reputation within the organization. The ombudsman's designation is much like a badge of honour.

The person chosen as ombudsman should have a sterling, almost charismatic, reputation within the organization.

It is a recognition of the fact that the person chosen is widely acknowledged within the organization for excellence in a mainstream specialization of the company. In addition, such a person is also expected to possess valuable people-oriented skills.

The ombudsman too should treat his position as an elevation, even though it may not carry any financial remuneration. Neither should the ombudsman's job be a full-time one. A good ombudsman is rarely a full-time ombudsman. There could be times when he might have to spend longer hours, and there could also be occasions when such a demanding schedule is not required.

There are many similarities between the ombudsman of today and the traditional leopard skin chief among the Nuers of East Africa (see Evans-Pritchard 1969). The leopard skin chief's job was not full-time either. Ordinarily this person carried on with his life like any other Nuer. This largely meant tending cattle and occasional agriculture. But the leopard skin chief came into his own when there was a dispute and the parties wanted a quick and amicable resolution.

When the leopard skin chief was asked to intervene in such matters he would don his leopard skin and become something like our modern ombudsman. The discussions would be held in his hut and the decision would be binding on both parties. Once the dispute was settled, the leopard skin chief sloughed off his loose leopard skin and became a Nuer cattle-raiser once again.

For the traditional leopard skin chief to accomplish his role successfully he needed to be widely accepted by his tribe. Neither force nor fear, but good, solid reputation built over years gave him the credibility for the job. Members of his tribe could relate to him and he to them. He belonged to the same company and in normal times he did what the ordinary Nuer was expected to do.

The Nuer people were somewhat unique in anthropological literature. They did not have any formal government or chieftainship. For this reason anthropologists call the Nuer society acephalous, or 'headless'. In spite of being without a king, chief, or president, Nuers were able to resolve conflicts amongst them with remarkable ease. The leopard skin chief, who acted as the chief negotiator in all major disputes, did not surround himself with the pomp of office, but functioned largely on trust and goodwill.

Against this background it is much clearer now why an ombudsman can be effective only when the person has an intrinsic legitimacy within the organization. An ombudsman's office should not strike awe but respect and trust. To be able to freely air your suspicions, anxieties, and fears, and to expect to get some solace, comfort, and solution in return, your ombudsman must be someone you can look up to. You don't want a law-and-order martinet, or an outsider who lacks empathy.

This is what makes the ombudsman seem more akin to the leopard skin chief than to the big boys of HRD or the professional consultant. A successful ombudsman does not depend on traditional methods of coercion, nor on the stated hierarchy, or pecking order, to draw respect. As ethical behaviour functions best on mutual respect and transparency, today's ombudsmen would do well to learn from the ways of simple people in distant lands.

In the final analysis, that ombudsman is the best ombudsman who wears a leopard skin under his pinstripe suit.

CHAPTER SEVEN

WALKING THE TALK

A Little Ethics Is a Dangerous Thing

Church on Sunday

'Church on Sunday, sin on Monday,' is a comfortable enough arrangement. From the looks of it even the real world conspires to make any other option practically unworkable. After all, even nice people like us have to survive. It is not as if we have a compulsive desire to grease palms, subvert the law, and cash in on every loophole, far from it! But if we do not do it somebody else will.

The fault then does not lie with us. What a relief! Well, okay, pass me the sin, please. To survive in this bad world every good bone in our bodies must morph into some kind of demonic lever. It is either that or quits. If we do not join the rat race we might as well move in with the church mouse next Sunday. Haven't we all heard that good guys come last?

Persuasive as this argument might sound it actually stems from a refusal to look ourselves straight in the eye and take responsibility for who we are and what we do. To blame it on others—our society, and even our culture—is patently a soft option. Bad ethics is really a sissy act for people who refuse to stand up and be counted.

To imagine a world without temptations for the short cut and quick buck is unreal. Yet there are many people out there who actually play by the rules. Indeed, without them, civil life, as we know it, would have been impossible. Both these options are equally real, but they involve different sets of interpersonal relations. There is little reason then why one sort of reality must be accepted as a fact of nature, and the other with a broad smile.

Unethical practice in a business organization begins with vulnerability at home to temptations outside. Such openings exist when there is a lack of clarity amongst employees regarding what is unacceptable, and what will not be tolerated at any cost.

Thus if an organization has *not* taken an informed and consensual decision as to what constitutes padding of expense accounts, or what the criteria for measuring success should be, or what makes for improper use of office facilities, then it is sitting on a tinder box. In the short run, issues of this sort do not seem to matter. Ambiguity in such cases may even be encouraged in the name of flexibility and quick results. Quite clearly, it is laxity at home that leaves a company's flanks wide open to unethical pressures from the outside. Or take the example of Enron where there was a refusal to walk the talk but just mouth core value with utter cynicism. It is probably hard to believe that Enron had listed its core values as Respect, Integrity, Community and Excellence (or RICE). This is an archetypal example of a nonfunctional ethical statement and it brought collective grief to Enron, Andersen, and many other small and large shareholders.

It is laxity at home that leaves a company's flanks wide open to unethical pressures from outside.

Ethics Is Not Just Compliance

Business Ethics is therefore not simply about making sure that everyone behaves, and that there is greater compliance. One needs to understand—compliance to what? Are the rules and norms spelt out so that they have general comprehensibility and consent? Research undertaken by DePaul University, Chicago has come up with conclusive evidence to show that companies that make a public commitment to ethics achieve significantly higher performance standards than those that do not. In other words, by making an ethical pledge to relevant stakeholders, a company significantly boosts its bottom line. This is also confirmed by the Stern Stewart analysis of Market Value Added (MVA), the *Fortune* magazine analysis of the most admired companies, and by the rankings put out by *Business Week* in the US. Research on 500 of the largest American corporations shows that the top 14 per cent distinguished themselves by making an explicit public commitment to ethics.

These findings all point to one overwhelming conclusion. Employees, as relevant stakeholders of a company, perform at higher levels once it is clear to them that their top management is committed to certain ethical values. These ethical values spell out the cultural specifics of an organization. They define the company and set it apart from others. The employees, staff and management wear these distinctive company traits and characteristics like a badge of honour. Once they commit themselves to the core ethical values of the company, discipline and compliance follow naturally.

Now the bad news: when the ethics programme of a company emphasizes compliance rather than values, it does more harm than good. In a compliance-based ethical programme, hierarchy, rules and sanctions assume dominant positions. There is little or no mention of *When a company emphasizes compliance rather than values, it does more harm than good.* core company values that underlie such compliance requirements.

Naturally, employees and staff see compliance-based ethics as yet another form of managerial control, and also perhaps as a ploy to shield top management from close scrutiny. Consequently, there is greater cynicism and a lower degree of commitment among workers and employees of a firm. In which case, clearly, it is better to do away with the ethical programme altogether. A little ethics, like a little learning, can be a dangerous thing.

Business Ethics really works best when there is a clear and transparent adherence to values at all levels within an organization. It is up to the senior management to demonstrate that not only are they serious about holding on to core values, but that it is equally important for them that these values manifest themselves in every department, level and function in the company. Only then is ethical accountability possible and, with it, greater enthusiasm towards work down the line.

Given the importance that Business Ethics is receiving in leading corporate circles, many companies feel that they too should be able to boast of an ethical programme. In a large number of cases, such ethical posturing is merely tokenism of one sort or another. These organizations might become members of the Ethics Officers Association as in the US, or put up a large signboard in their establishments loudly proclaiming high moral values. Or, as is most often the case, their annual reports are prefixed with solemn ethical platitudes.

Yet, token ethics and compliance-based ethics only draw derision and contempt from the rank and file of workers. They see it as so much window dressing. Naturally, such weak-kneed approaches to ethics do more harm than good to company morale.

If an organization is not willing to go the distance, then it is best that it scrap ethics altogether. In such cases it is probably better not to have an ethical programme at all. This is the moral of the story.

To be effective, Business Ethics demands, over and above a resolute will at the top to clean up one's own backyard, a set of pre-eminent values that are thoughtfully concretized in terms of actual office procedure. This is the real test of walking the talk. It is this that will give practical demonstration of the top executives' commitment to seal off areas of vulnerability within the organization and not to suffer them in the name of flexibility, profit, or individual initiative. Naturally, as we are in a constantly changing world, where new threats emerge unbeknown to most of us, periodic risk assessments are necessary which would then force into the open the organization's many implicit norms. Some of them may be excellent but there may be several others that have to be shown the door.

If an organization is not willing to go the distance, then it is best that it scrap ethics altogether.

Enter the 'Fixer', the Sycophant

A full-fledged ethics programme cannot only be compliance-oriented — it should undertake periodic risk assessments as well. The truth is that if such risk assessments are not made it will be the wrong kind of enterprise that will take over. The 'fixer', the commission seeker, and the smooth talker will gradually gain prominence within the organization. Before long the trusted lieutenant will be turning the knife deep into the

organization's innards pleading helplessness against the forces of a corrupt world.

Beware of this breed; they take pleasure in making you do wrong and profit from it, but get away scot-free while you suffer the consequences.

Sycophants are not just disgusting creatures, they are harmful too. All the sweet talk, the lavish praise, and the permanent oily smile are actually aimed at helping you commit your first small sin. The flatterer would like to hold your hand firmly when you take that initial short step, assuring you all the while that there is simply nothing wrong in what you are doing.

After this small first sin the flatterer has you in the pocket. This smooth talker will gradually take you on to doing bigger things without you ever suspecting that anything is amiss. A successful sycophant gradually changes the way in which the targeted subject thinks. Slowly a new thought pattern takes over. Dependence, excessive narcissism, and eventually a kind of recklessness on all fronts, characterize a mind that is in the thrall of flattery.

A successful sycophant gradually changes the way in which the targeted subject thinks.

As a corollary to all this, successful sycophants also create problems which only they can resolve. The flattered, on the other hand, ends up being so wound up and enamoured with the self that the thought that there could be an error in judgement never occurs, however fleetingly. In this overheated sense of self-glow all the seeds that the flatterer sows take root as if in a personalized greenhouse. As every wrongdoing begets another, sycophants soon appear to be indispensable. They alone have the key to the problems you are up against, till at the end the organization is being run on proxy.

But none of this ever comes through blatantly. This is because the sycophant works on altering other people's psyche. The flattered begin to fancy themselves with such exaggeration that they just cannot believe that they have been had. Thus even when the going gets tough it is the hapless object of empty flattery who takes the rap while the sycophant gets away scot-free. There is nothing that would incriminate that slick smooth talker. The flatterer only pulled the strings on somebody else's vulnerable ego while remaining carefully guarded from view.

Sycophancy can be dangerous not just to the person who is at the receiving end of the flattery but also to the organization as a whole. Sycophants always choose their victims carefully. They must necessarily be people in power who have the authority to take sensitive decisions without being questioned too closely. Such people usually have a fairly wide area of discretionary privileges. It is then left to the sycophant's persuasive abilities to convert what is discretionary into arbitrary acts of self-will. Moreover, sycophancy encourages an organizational culture that undermines hard work and true enterprise.

The unctuous counsel of the sycophant does not seem self-serving at first blush. Some may even pity sycophants for the many acts of genuflection and self-debasement that they routinely perform. Sycophants might seem to be stoking somebody else's ego, but in actual fact they are feathering their own nest at the expense of the whole enterprise. Though a sycophant may be spotted by the naked eye by almost everybody who is not in the charmed circle of the flattered ego, yet even they seldom realize that the sycophant is damaging the organization and not just puffing up a single individual.

The reach of systematic flattery is much wider than just propping up the designated object of attention. Bit by bit, and slowly but surely, the sycophant robs the organization of its systems of checks and balances, and of its sense of propriety and fairness. It is therefore critical to be able to spot the effects of sycophancy before it is too late. There should also be mechanisms in place that can alert those in senior positions that a sycophant is at work. A successful sycophant will usually be a member of a large number of committees, well beyond what is the average for the company. Obviously, the sycophant will then be in positions for which he lacks the necessary competence.

Sycophancy is dangerous not just to the person it targets but to the organization as a whole.

One way or another, a sycophant succeeds in breaking office protocol and encourages a personalized decision-making style. A successful sycophant has an extraordinarily long tenure at the same desk while others are being shuffled and transferred. The status of that desk keeps getting elevated with fancier titles and better pay. Sycophants rarely ever ask for leave as they are having just a great time in the office anyway.

As it is not easy to resist a flatterer, it is necessary to put systems in place that discourage sycophants from working their charm. Also be ready to recognize red flags when they pop up even if that makes you look a little foolish.

The Pastoral Entrepreneur

A further tip on how to walk the talk, with head held high, is to hypothetically imagine oneself in the shoes of a person who has been betrayed because adequate checks were not in place. Only then the importance of implementing Business Ethics in one's organization will become clear, in a truly intersubjective way. It is often very difficult to put oneself in another person's shoes and see the world from that perspective. There are vast dissimilarities in education, upbringing, kinship structures, and so forth. But Business Ethics, as we have pointed out repeatedly, is not something that happens naturally. It is a cultivated disposition, deliberately arrived at, because it takes into account the long-term interests of stakeholders. To drive home this point starkly let us think what it would be like if we were at the receiving end of a corporate fraud.

Unlike small-time sharks and skinflint traders, world-class players are actively concerned about customer welfare. That business has a pastoral role to play is not something that is being added on. It is in the nature of legitimate enterprise itself. There is a social duty that all businesses must fulfil for long-term success, whether or not customers come growling to their doorsteps.

There is a social duty all businesses must fulfil for long-term success.

Much too often the pastoral aspect of business is overlooked. It is as if corporate enterprises are only money-spinning machines. An important reason why modern enterprise took off in the West is because the concern with the ordinary citizen was much stronger there than elsewhere. Only when democracy and capitalism joined forces was the stagnant feudal order in Europe overwhelmed. Thereafter, as democracy got stronger, so did capitalism. Spoilt members of the old nobility could not take advantage of their position to leverage their way into the modern age. They were incapable of respecting people for who they were. After all, markets cannot flourish at gunpoint, nor can goods find buyers by authoritative decrees.

If India is still struggling to be an important economic force it is because the pastoral spirit and the democratic temperament are not yet well entrenched in our society. When tigers die attempts are made to clear the zoo officials. When buildings collapse erring contractors bribe their way out of trouble. Producers of substandard goods and spurious drugs get away because most of their victims cannot strike back. Naturally, under these circumstances, to paraphrase Gresham's law, bad eggs will drive out the good. More and more entrepreneurs will feel that the only way to prosper is to lie, cheat and bend every law in the book. This can only hurt the long-term interests of the corporate sector in this country.

Perhaps in some areas of corporate life a strong consumer awareness has not developed. In many instances, adequate laws might not exist thus allowing buccaneer bourgeoisie to indulge themselves by exploiting other peoples' vulnerability. Even so, a long-term strategist would see the dangers inherent in killing the tiger in us, for the tiger could easily have been you.

99.44 Per Cent Honesty

Accepting that dishonesty is out, is there a golden rule on how to be honest? What happens when different long-cherished principles conflict with each other? Can one be equally honest to each one of those principles, or is some adjustment called for?

Ivory Soap is declared to be 99.44 per cent pure, but as a soap it does its job very well. Perhaps there is a lesson in this for Business Ethics.

The big question therefore is whether 100 per cent honesty is the best way to fight dishonesty, or should one aim for 99.44 per cent honesty instead?

Is it advisable to be 100 per cent honest or 99.44 per cent honest?

Examine the following issues, do a little test for yourself, keep the results confidential if you wish, but please do act on them.

Robert F. Bohn, past president of the Academy of Financial Services in US, opts for 99.44 per cent honesty rather than 100 per cent honesty. He argues that being a little less than 100 per cent honest allows greater room for integrity in practice. A mechanical 100 per cent endorsement of honesty can be quite thoughtless of the human condition and of the complexities that a context might produce.

Is this argument correct?

Let us recall the differences of opinion between Socrates and his favourite disciple, Plato. For Socrates the truth could not be diluted on any account. Plato, occasionally, would like truth to be nuanced. For example, Plato argued that if a person had borrowed a knife from a deranged friend it was in the best interest of all concerned to conceal the knife and not return it to its rightful owner.

Imagine a scenario where a super speciality company is facing temporary difficulties in realizing payments and is hence forced to delay giving out increments to its highly skilled employees for two months. Under these conditions what should the top management do? Reveal to its employees the truth of how company finances stand at that point of time, and perhaps trigger off unrest and even job turnovers? Or, would it be advisable instead to tell the employees that there has been only a minor oversight, and that the money would come to them very soon? As there is no real crisis the company could even announce the increments though they would not be paid just yet. This alternative would save employees unnecessary anxieties and also keep the company working on an even keel.

A young worker with potential has joined your company. This person may be nervous and could foul up the first assignment. Should one be perfectly honest and shred whatever self-esteem there is left in the new recruit or help boost the young colleague's confidence with a few tactful dishonesties?

On such occasions can 99.44 per cent honesty come to our help?

It must also be remembered that in all such cases 99.44 per cent honesty is a delicate balance. Where does one draw the line? At what point does a little less than 100 per cent honesty begin to do more harm than good?

The Ethical Rule of Thumb

As has already become very evident, the most difficult problems to resolve are always the small ones. Every now and again corporate executives are faced with a niggling dilemma and they wish they had a rough and ready way to find their way out of the quandary.

For example, is it alright to post some of your depart-ment's earnings of the current year to next year because the business outlook for the coming months is not all that promising? That way you would look good in front of the board while everybody else would appear incom-petent. Is it permissible to use your office service pro-vider to set up your home computer or cooling system? Is it alright to have your company sponsor an event in which your child is participating?

The law is silent on these matters, and that is just as well. But these are ethical dilemmas for which each organization must find adequate answers, such that it is able to develop a common policy on these issues. Every now and then though a new dilemma crops up for which executives are not quite prepared. In such cases a rule of thumb would certainly be handy.

But what would be that rule of thumb?

I have often heard it being said that if a certain decision does not entail a monetary loss for the company then it is okay to go ahead with it. For example, the firm loses nothing if the dealer puts your daughter in a school of your choice. Nor would the firm suffer financially when you push back your earnings for this year to the next. Neither are you making off with company funds if your travel agent can exchange your entitlement to a business class ticket in such a way that now you and your spouse can travel together by paying economy fare. So where does the problem lie?

In all such cases, even though the company is not losing any money, a bad precedent has been set. The integrity of records has been tampered with, and *It is the first wrong step that is the most critical on most occasions.*

once this starts who knows where it will stop. It is the first wrong step that is the most critical on most occasions.

A good rule of thumb could well be to imagine what it would be like if the act you are contemplating were to appear as headline news in the morning papers. Would you be able to face the world? Your friends? Your subordinates? Your colleagues? Your family?

If you can, then go ahead; but if you cannot, stop right there!

This rule of thumb can help in moments of emergency, but obviously it cannot be the recommended policy for long-term organizational behaviour. In order to sort out ethical dilemmas one has to think more self-consciously in terms of 'ethical dilemma workshops' which were discussed in Chapter 3.

The Rumour Industry

In most cases rumours take off because ethical dilemmas have not been dealt with satisfactorily. This means in practice that there are different laws for different people. It is difficult to exaggerate the importance of resolving ethical dilemmas in an institutionalized fashion, for this is the best opportunity senior management has for feedback on how good their vision statements and their codes of conduct are.

It is true that at times gossip can be healthy, but not rumour.

Several studies suggest that a savvy chief executive officer can get a lot of information about the company by tapping into local gossip. Though not always 100 per cent fool proof, gossip usually has a fairly high credibility index.

There is that occasional exaggeration, that extra sting in the tail, but on the whole gossip in the shop tells one a lot about the shop itself. Top management would do well to pay attention to this gossip and swing into action every time they hear a rumour.

Gossip can be healthy, but rumours are destructive.

Rumours too are spread by wagging tongues but, unlike gossip, breed on lack of information. Under the communist regime, Russia was notorious for all kinds of rumours. Rumours spread panic, and are generally subversive in character. The only way to keep rumours out and gossip in is to allow for free flow of information. In short, be transparent.

Rumours usually thrive when the company, or even the industry, is going through a period of crisis. When big changes are imminent and not many people know how to make sense of them, the tendency at the top is usually to button up. This could be one strategy, but it is certainly not the best one. As bad news can hardly be quarantined it is more advisable to be open about impending transformations and the possible choices ahead. This would certainly lower the level of anxiety all around and put brakes on the rumour mills that are rearing to go.

But gossip is not nearly as destructive. Occasionally, it lets you in on who the laggards are; who are those who want to be the boss's favourite; who are the quiet, silent types; and so forth. It can also give senior management an inside view of what it is to work in a certain department or on a certain shift. The foreman, or the manager in charge, on the other hand, may coat the routine report with the kind of sugar he thinks his boss would like. Accessing gossip therefore gives another dimension that official reviews do not often throw up. It can be a vital kind of upward information.

But how can senior management access gossip? By establishing common lunch facilities, encouraging cross-level recreational activities, and holding periodic workshops on company policy and direction. All such initiatives require a lot of careful deliberation before they can be put into practice; but they are worth it.

Remember, only good gossip can drive out bad rumours.

Exit Polls

Another method for tapping into information that might be crucial, and certainly useful to curb rumours, is to speak to those who are leaving. They have little to lose and will give you valuable feedback about your enterprise and issues at work.

The person who leaves your company and goes elsewhere should not be treated like a pariah, but as a very valuable information source. Every *An employee leaving* psephologist will tell you that the most *your company can* reliable information about voting *give you important* patterns can be accessed through exit *insights.* polls, that is as the voter is leaving the voting booth. Likewise, it is the employee who leaves your company who will, in all likelihood, be truthful about what is right and wrong with

your organization. Some of what is said may be unfair—
it is also likely that the person could be putting on an
act and boasting, but even so pay attention. This is another exit poll, the corporate exit poll, if you please, and
it can yield valuable information.

The usual reaction to an employee who finds a job elsewhere is to try and forget the incident as quickly as possible. Rarely does such a person get a polite send-off
with the concurrence of those who are senior in rank.
An employee who has chosen to leave cannot be of the
right sort, so why waste time pressing flesh, or even
worse, listen to what this man or woman may have to
say? More often than not, however, this runaway recruit
will have a number of admirers, especially among those
who are at the same level and below. If this is the case,
the management certainly ought to know. It does not
portend well for the company that the exiting person
should leave behind so many heaving with envy.

There are many reasons why a person may choose to
go elsewhere. What those at the top often tend to overlook is that when a person quits there is a certain amount
of disquiet in the ranks. It is therefore important to be
able to effectively address those who stay behind. This
is where an exit poll is essential. Sometimes better pay
is a reason for quitting, but what does this salary increase
amount to? Rs 3,000/5,000/10,000? This too is worth
knowing. If the difference is not very substantial then
in all likelihood it may be something else besides the
obvious monetary reason. In my opinion if the person
is leaving for up to a 10–15 per cent increase in pay, the
problem lies elsewhere and not in a few pieces of silver.

In a large number of instances employees leave because
they find a more challenging job elsewhere. This too is

necessary for the senior management to know. If those who love to be challenged are quitting, then obviously the conditions of work aren't testing their skills to the limit. To stem the tide of the best and the brightest from going elsewhere it is important that facilities be made available to upgrade their skills and then to help them deploy these new techniques at work. This obviously implies that the pressure is on those at the top to constantly innovate — both at the product and at the process stage. So if the exit poll indicates that people are leaving because the other job is 'more interesting' or 'more fun', it would be wise to read these statements as 'the job here is getting boring and dull'.

The exit poll may also show that employees often panic and leave because they misread some signals in the market. If this be the case then it is necessary for senior management to meet employees on a regular basis, especially during troubled times, and explain how the company is handling the crisis of the day, and how the market is affecting their line of work. This would certainly save the company a lot of unnecessary bother and prevent many employees from chasing after mirages. An exit poll can thus help both the top management and the employee.

It is difficult to say what the exit poll will come up with. But an ex-employee, even at the point of leaving, can do you a good turn and help you to convert a loss into an asset. A fond farewell, my friend, and thank you for the gossip! Many top executives realize the importance of these exit interviews. These interactions help in sorting out misunderstandings that could crop up in the future. Also, quite significantly, they help to make the higher levels of the organization more sensitive to rumblings on the ground, and thereby increase their accessibility across the company.

Know Your A.Q.

Accessibility to superiors promotes teamwork and contributes to greater efficiency. It releases energy and initiatives down the line. But how does one go about increasing the Accessibility Quotient (A.Q.) of an enterprise?

Accessibility to superiors releases energy and initiatives down the line.

The key to higher A.Q. in the corporate world is not back-slapping bonhomie. In fact too much of that might send confusing and contradictory signals. Decision-making is the responsibility of those at the top. Even so, accessibility demands that decision-makers be answerable for their decisions and that they factor inputs from below before they make up their minds.

Neither can high A.Q. levels be premised on the assumption that people spontaneously want to communicate honestly. Pure goodwill or trusting naiveté cannot guarantee ethical communication. To ensure ethical communication, and consequently, higher A.Q. levels, measures need to be adopted which would make dishonest communication harder to pull off, less credible, and subject to penalties.

There are at least three objective steps an organization can take to raise its A.Q.:

    i. *Downsizing Confidentiality.* An organization's A.Q. goes up when there is a clear, self-conscious and well-thought-out policy regarding what should be deemed 'confidential material'. Reducing areas of information that are routinely, often capriciously, shrouded in confidentiality would instantly raise the Accessibility Quotient of the organization.

ii. *Introducing Upward Assessment.* Contrary to the usual format, it is now subordinates who are evaluating the person they report to. Several large companies have already introduced this procedure. These assessments are not meant to embarrass superiors, but to help them perform better and more responsively.

iii. *Conducting Ethics Workshops.* Periodic workshops, with participants from different levels and functions, also help to raise A.Q. levels. These workshops must focus on critical ethical dilemmas that the company has faced in the recent past. This will increase the general awareness, and appreciation, of the constraints and limitations that management at different levels faces.

CHAPTER EIGHT

VENDOR MONITORING AND COMPLIANCE

A New Dimension of Business Ethics

Vendor monitoring involves hiring an independent agency by a company purchasing goods to ensure that its supplier complies with the agreed norms of production. The need for vendor monitoring arises when consumers demand that the goods they buy be produced under humane conditions and ethically acceptable standards. Many large companies have had to encounter customer wrath for selling goods that are associated, for example, with child labour. Consequently, they have faced serious problems in reviving their legitimacy in the marketplace.

Practically all vendor monitoring assignments involve purchasers from the West sourcing goods from Indian suppliers and poorer countries of Asia, Africa and Latin America. Hopefully, in due course of time, purchasers from these poorer countries too will be pressured by customers at home and will see the benefits of vendor monitoring.

Vendor monitoring was initially prompted by customer outrage when information came through that some of the goods sold in Western retail stores were produced by children. Gradually the scope of vendor monitoring widened to include the overall regime of wages and benefits as well as the working conditions prevailing in the suppliers' production facilities.

There is an umbilical connection between Business Ethics and vendor monitoring.

Vendor monitoring is related to Business Ethics because companies are now responsible to their customers not just in terms of quality and prices, but also in terms of social justice and fairness. No longer can any business organization, particularly in the West, pass the odium of poor working conditions and child labour onto its suppliers, without suffering a loss of credibility. It is the totality of the production process that counts with customers and not just the price value of the goods. Such awareness levels have led many companies, some of them very forward-looking, to make a public statement of their ethical policy. As a result they have allowed themselves to be judged on their business practices as transparently as possible by their customers and other stakeholders. It follows therefore that such companies need to assure themselves that their suppliers and subcontractors are not indulging in practices that would sully their reputation later in the eyes of their customers. Hence the umbilical connection between Business Ethics and vendor monitoring.

Global Attack on Child Labour

Globalization has brought many things in its wake (see *Appendix I*), and one of them is sensitivity towards child labour. Many established companies in the West were rocked when charges were levelled against them that their products were made with child labour. Nike, for one, moved swiftly to cleanse its reputation. It has now made sure, to the extent possible, that children touch none of its products before they are ready for sale.

As child labour robs children of their potential at a very early age, there is just opposition and outrage against it all over the world. Unfortunately, anti-child labour regulations rarely go any further. What is the next step after banishing child labour? How can children get a better life? The anti-child labour laws, which are largely inspired by the United Nations charter on the subject, make clear that any child under 14 is a child labourer. Child labour laws usually specify that the employment is illegal if the nature of employment hurts the

intellectual and physical development of children. There is still a lack of clarity in some countries regarding whether children who work at home are to be considered child labourers too (see Lieten 2002: 5191). This is not quite as simple as it seems for it has been noticed how children can be put to work at home in occupations that are potentially hazardous. *Beedi*-making is one such example (Government of India 1995). For this reason, vendor monitors must be clear about what the scope of their job is with respect to child labour.

Many Western purchasing houses, such as IKEA, are not satisfied with obeying the law as it stands, or finding refuge in its ambiguities. Rather they believe in pressing on with the spirit of the anti-child labour legislations. This often results in a more categorical judgement of child labour wherein even a child working at home to produce goods for the buyers is not permissible, unless there is good reason to believe that this is only a part-time activity and that the child also goes to school. The reason why these buyers are very strict on this issue is because they believe that all possible excuses for children labouring in centres producing for them should be sealed off. This is just the beginning, but there is still a lot that remains to be done on this issue.

It is not enough to ban child labour. The corporate sector needs to do much more.

Bangladesh, for example, has practically rid its garment units of child labour. However, it is not as if these children are in schools honing their talents for a more meaningful future. Nobody really knows what has happened to the thousands of children who were rendered jobless by the strictures on child labour imposed on Bangladesh by major Western buyers. It is suspected that many of them have taken to begging and worse.

This is not just the story of Bangladesh, but it applies to most parts of the developing world, India included. Child labour is rampant in all these countries, even if the suppliers of Nike or Macy's or Hudson's Bay or IKEA or Gap are now quite clean. In India child labour flourishes most egregiously in carpet-weaving, in the manufacturing of matchsticks and fireworks, as well as in the many eating establishments all over the country. Quite clearly, children are in large numbers in those industries that do not require its labour force to possess developed musculature or advanced technical skills.

The original incentive for employing children was obviously to lower the cost of production. Such crude cost reduction methods were clearly driven by competition, and we, as consumers, also benefited from these low prices. But the ability of consumers to determine prices is limited to the range that is actually available in the marketplace. This is why it is important that the state, and other important players, such as the corporate sector, step in to ensure that labour costs are not decreased to inhuman levels in the name of competition or cost cutting. Incidentally, this is how the first labour legislations found their way into statute books in Britain.

It is therefore in the fitness of things that external agencies insist that child labour be banned. This still does not, however, answer the question as to why parents send their children to work and not to school. Assuming that all parents think of the welfare of their children, how then could they go so drastically wrong?

The gruelling circumstances of poverty rob people of long-term rationality. Seen in this context we realize that long-term planning is a luxury that only some can afford. When the next meal is the uppermost consideration, there is little or no scope for planning for the future. The future in most poverty-stricken homes is the next minute. In families where infant mortality stalks with relentless vigour the one thought that stamps out all is how to keep the child alive. It is a shocking statistic that children under five account for 75 per cent of deaths in India. Under such conditions, it does not come as a surprise that parents in dire poverty encourage their children to earn a living instead of sending them to school.

Taking children off garment and carpet industries is simply not enough. They would not have been there in the first place if their parents could afford something better. To agitate against child labour without finding adequate facilities for upgrading the lives of these children borders on hypocrisy. It is indeed a shame that even those enterprises that can afford to go further and really help children earn a better future are satisfied with merely taking children off the employment register. It is also shameful that those morally outraged customers in the West who pointed a finger at Nike are unconcerned about what happens to the children once they are fired from work.

It is shameful that even Western customers are unconcerned about what happens to children once they are fired from work.

Eventually the task of educating children rests upon the state. Others can only make a contribution towards it. The corporate sector can help in this effort in a variety of ways. It can raise funds specially earmarked for this purpose. It can also insist that its suppliers conform to minimal wage levels that would allow their employees to send their children to school. In this connection, major buyers from the West can also play a significant role. They have the economic power to force those units from whom they source products to give adequate proof of their contribution towards children's education.

Anti-child labour laws become truly relevant when accompanied by active programmes to educate and develop potentialities latent among children. IKEA, along with UNICEF, runs a large project covering 500 villages in the carpet belt of U.P. with just this aim in mind. Failing this approach all exhortations against child labour are mere chatter and posturing. If banning child labour could eradicate poverty, strictures on it are on target. But if child labour is on account of poverty, and not the other way round, then are we not mistaking the symptom for the cause?

It is just too glib to believe that once child labour is eradicated poverty will automatically recede. This view ultimately rests on the superior assumption that people from poor backgrounds do not have their children's best interests at heart; that they cruelly send their little ones to work when they could easily have gone to school. Once this hidden assumption is spelt out, its untenability becomes obvious. Which parent would like such a fate to stalk his or her children? If the adult labour force in a poor country had sufficient bargaining power to get a decent wage and support their children, surely child labour would not be an issue.

It is just too glib to believe that once child labour is eradicated poverty will automatically recede.

Bold policy measures to free children from the drudgery of sweatshops do not, however, come easily. When the anti-child labour policies were being contemplated in

England they met with a lot of resistance from poor families who felt that the earnings from their children were now being denied to them. In fact one mother said to the Royal Commission enquiring into child labour in mines: 'I went to the pit myseif when I was five years old, and two of my daughters go there now. It does them no harm. It did me no harm' (Report on Mines, vol. XVI, 1842, p. 27; quoted in Young and Willmott 1973: 74). The freeing of child labour is therefore an enlightened policy act that must be accompanied by other measures such as housing, education, and health. In England, anti-child labour laws were enforced with the Act of 1893 (see Hobhouse 1994: 42), but not as a stand-alone measure. The beneficial effects of banning child labour can be seen in Britain today.

If consumer power could get the advanced world worked up against child labour, it should now be possible for the corporate sector in these countries to wrest the initiative and go the distance. It's the pacesetter in the pack that always gains the most. Let the children of the world truly benefit from globalization.

Compliance is More Than Banning Child Labour

That most Western buyers are dominated by anti-child labour concern is very interesting in itself. There isn't equal zealousness in many cases in monitoring issues such as those related to hours of work, union representation, working conditions, overtime wages, maternity leave, or health care. This allows the management in garment units and other supplier enterprises to flog workers for well over the legal limit of 60 hours a week. In some cases the workers put in as many as 17 straight hours of work in a day, particularly in the garment industry, during the peak months between November and February. The stipulation that one full day should be given as a holiday in a week is not always adhered to either.

Yet, given the extreme poverty of these workers, there is very little protest against such long hours. Extra work means overtime pay. Even if the overtime wages are most often dishonestly calculated, they still represent a very valued amount of money for these poor workers. In fact, the high rate of turnover of workers in the garment industry is because they are constantly in search of units that will give them more hours of overtime work. This enables Western buyers to drive prices down and be competitive at home. This also allows the owners of these manufactories to meet targets at short notice.

Most supplier units fault on working conditions and environmental concerns.

That most of these supplier units in the developing world fault on overtime payments, health care, and maternity leave is somehow not newsworthy. These issues do not catch the public's imagination the way child labour does. From the point of view of the suppliers, employing a child instead of an adult is no big saving anyway. If the hours of work can be stretched, if over-time wages can be reduced, if health and welfare payments do not have to be made, then why should the management complain against strictures on child labour? The only way this bluff could be called is if there was a respectable consumer movement across the world that would act in concert to pressure buyers to make sure that suppliers adhere to the full compliance package which includes working conditions and environmental concerns. Needless to say, the garment workers themselves are too poor and disorganized to be able to assert their rights on their own. This is where Globalization can play a positive role.

CHAPTER NINE

GLOBALIZATION AND THE PARADIGM SHIFT

From Production to Consumption

Cynics might say: So what is so new about globalization? In a way they are right. Capitalism has never respected national boundaries from its earliest days. World wars and trade wars have been common enough occurrences for the last hundred years and more. At the same time it has also been noticed that technical innovations have not stopped at the frontiers of a nation, nor have fads and fashions. So what is novel about globalization? Is it just another word?

What globalization brings to the table is a new ideological shift. This is clearly visible in the manner in which businesses are projected today. In this era trade unions have been laid low and along *Globalization* with them the emphasis on production and *has made the* producers as the main planks of economic *consumer* thought and policy-making. In their place *pivotal to all* the consumer has stepped in and has become *calculations.* pivotal to all calculations. If the customer wants a product it must be made available. Economic restrictions and trade policies that earlier determined what would be produced, and how, are now looked upon with distaste.

In the age when production was central, technologies entered only if they first cleared national barriers regarding what was to be produced. Today, consumers get the first preference and any obstruction towards getting these goods and services across to them is anathema to the ideology of globalization. This makes the consumer king in the age of globalization.

In other words economic policies centre around what consumers want. It is no longer material if the production of these items brings about unemployment, greater economic dependency, or lack of trade union privileges. These issues mattered a great deal in the earlier age that was production-centric. National well-being and economic sovereignty were critical issues then that could not be ignored; indeed, they had to be kept upfront in any policy formulation. This approach quite logically led to planned and centralized development in which workers' rights, wages, wage goods, and production conditions were critical considerations.

This regime of production favoured an ideology that privileged economic independence and sovereignty at the national level above profit-making calculations. According to this point of view it was essential that each country be economically strong and self-reliant so that it could bargain from a position of strength. This rationale was factored in very consciously and with high ideological fervour. Therefore if the long-term interest of the nation meant that cars of a certain kind, or colour televisions and fuzzy logic washing machines, would not be produced because that might jeopardize a country's economic self-reliance, then so be it. Decisions regarding production were tied umbilically to national development and sovereignty.

Once the emphasis is on what is to be produced, it naturally entails that producers and production methods gain a high degree of salience in economic affairs. Technology should not be of the kind that induces dependence either. So what was produced depended upon skills that could be internally generated. This would ensure that a nation's overall economic sovereignty in a highly competitive international world order would not be compromised. In this climate, making profits became secondary. Even capitalists were shamefaced about the profits they made. Stagnant production methods were unfortunately justified in the name of economic sovereignty. This allowed permitocrats, trade unions and hand-picked capitalists to do rather well in a closed market.

If the ideology of globalization is now on the ascendant it is largely because earlier production-centred economies ran out of steam a few decades after they were introduced. They were mired in corruption and quite unable to free themselves from bureaucratese. It was not at all surprising then that the rationale behind production-oriented economies fell into disfavour at the popular level. Globalization emerged against this background to fill the ideological vacuum. It is not as if the call for globalization emerged only lately. It was always there and was championed by the advanced capitalist countries. It was the underdeveloped world that was resisting it so far.

Production may not be a dominant ideological leverage any longer, but it cannot be altogether dismissed from realistic economic decision-making. The difference that globalization has brought about is not that it has made production concerns immaterial, but that the leading factor is now the consumer and production must do what it can to meet the demands of the market. So every now and again one comes up against serious production problems at the national level that can only be resolved at the global level by importing skills or machinery.

Production may not be a dominant ideological leverage any longer, but it cannot be altogether dismissed from realistic economic decision-making.

Thus while it is true that consumer tastes are getting more visible and homogenized across the world, production facilities have not quite kept up. Economic difficulties at the national level arise from this mismatch.

Capital, to repeat an old truism, only moves to satisfy those consumer needs where there is profit to be made. Consequently consumerism is best manifested at higher expenditure levels. Production techniques are then geared to meet these demands regardless of what is required by the less privileged classes, or what they can reasonably afford. Thus we have a spate of super-specialized hospitals, but the existing national health care systems are in serious trouble. Likewise with educational institutions and transportation systems. The government agencies that provided for these facilities are hopelessly inadequate, but there is no public outcry because of this.

Today there is a greater discussion about getting multiple brands of cars in the market, but not nearly that much enthusiasm for public transport. It is as if there is a real and a vicarious market for consumerism. There are those who have been there and done that over and over again, and then there are those who are fantasizing about possessing consumer articles, even if in their shabbier and less glitzy versions.

Consumerism is still not a mass phenomenon in the poorer regions of the globe. Most people in such societies cannot afford the luxury of indulging in full-blooded consumerism, no matter how passionately their hearts may long for it. Their economic wherewithal rarely matches up to their consumerist needs. The West has been historically more fortunate in this regard. Consumerism came about as a result of advanced capitalism. In countries like India where the process has been telescoped quite dramatically, and where there is a small class of true consumers, globalization has to rely on the very long-run trickle-down effect for consumerism to gain a wider social base. As planned production-centred economies failed to deliver in the first round, attention is increasingly focussed on how to satisfy end users of any product. This is the ideological shift.

Of course, to a large extent, it is over 50 years of experience that took the shine off the producerist regime, largely because it was attended by corruption and red-tapism. There is also the element of impatience—people had waited long to have their aspirations realized and were no longer willing to put things on hold for the distant ideals of economic sovereignty. Also, well after five decades of post colonial statehood, the dread of becoming a subject nation again through the back door of economic control appeared less and less convincing.

There is a quite discernible demand growing at the popular level not just for consumer items but also for skills that will help in getting them. Those who had once campaigned against English language as a medium of school instruction in India would find themselves in a dreadful minority today. Poor villagers and socially backward classes want education to extricate themselves from the past so that they can confidently meet the future. This is also an aspect of consumerism except we are not talking of goods directly but how to get to them. Not just education, other public goods such as health, transport and energy are equally sought after across classes without paying as much attention to who is providing them but rather to the fact that they should be available to the user. The ideologies of yore appear tired and irrelevant now as they did not centralize consumer satisfaction.

It is true that countries like India have a long way to go before public goods at quality levels can be easily accessed, but one can see how people in general are reaching out to them even when governments falter in delivering them. As one moves from the issue of public goods to consumer products there is a similar, perhaps more pronounced, urge to acquire. Because producer-ism ideologies have few takers, national boundaries are becoming less relevant so long as the consumers get what they want. The positive side is that some aspects of advanced consumer consciousness in the west are making their way to developing countries in this process.

This impact is being felt in areas such as social auditing and compliance reporting. Because of the insistence of consumers worldwide, local suppliers of international purchasers have to raise standards in terms of conditions and hours of production, not to mention observing strictures against child labour. Many of these suppliers in the developing countries had never heard of such guidelines before. In this way the merchant mentalities of these small entrepreneurs are gradually being transformed towards greater professionalism.

Now nobody really thought of re-tooling the merchant supplier into a professional entrepreneur. But with the emphasis shifting to the consumer and the end-user, national blockages against international capital have been dropped enabling advanced consumer conscious-ness to come in along with foreign investments. The unintended consequence of this is the enlarged scope for introducing ethical principles even in humble sup-plier production sites in small towns and villages. Imagine if each foreign buyer representing a large brand name like IKEA, GAP, Nike or Walmart insists on com-pliance standards down their supply chain where there are literally thousands of producers across the country, in towns and villages, what a catalytic impact that will have on the manufacturing industries nation-wide.

BIBLIOGRAPHY

Berlin, Isiah, 1981, *Against the Current: Essays in the History of Ideas* (Oxford: Oxford University Press).

Blanchard, Ken, 1987, 'Managing By Values', in Ken Shelton (ed.), *Integrity at Work* (Utah: Executive Excellence Publications).

Coase, R.H., 1937, 'The Nature of the Firm', *Economica*, Vol. 4, pp. 368–405.

Deal, Terence and Allan A. Kennedy, 1982, *Corporate Cultures: The Rites and Rituals of Corporate Life* (Reading, Massachusetts: Perseus Press).

Donaldson, T. and L.E. Preston, 1995, 'The Stakeholder Theory of the Corporation: Concepts, Evidence, Implications', *Academy of Management Review*, Vol. 20, pp. 65–91.

Elias, Norbert, 1978, *The Civilizing Process*, Vol. 1, *The History of Manners* (New York: Pantheon).

Evans-Pritchard, E.E., 1969, *The Nuer* (Oxford: Oxford University Press).

Friedman, Milton, 1987, *The Essence of Friedman* (California: Stanford University Press).

Government of India, 1995, *Unorganized Sector Services: Report on the Working and Living Conditions of Beedi Industry in India* (Chandigarh/Shimla: Ministry of Labour).

Hartman, Laura Pincus, 1998, *Perspectives in Business Ethics*, Management and Organization Series (Singapore: McGraw-Hill International Editions).

Harvard Business Review on Leadership, 1998 (Boston: Harvard University Press).

Hobhouse, L.T., 1994, *Liberalism and Other Writings* (Cambridge: Cambridge University Press).

Kant, Immanuel, 1983, *Perpetual Peace and Other Essays in Politics, History and Morals* (Indianapolis: Hackett Publishing Company).

Kaptein, Muel, 1998, *Ethics Management: Auditing and Developing the Ethical Content of Organizations* (Dodrecht, The Netherlands: Kluwer Academic Publishers).

Krygier, Martin, 1997, *Between Fear and Hope: Hybrid Thoughts on Public Values*, Boyer Lectures (Sydney: Australia Broadcasting Corporation).

Lieten, G.K., 2002, 'Child Labour in India: Disentangling Essence and Solutions,' *Economic and Political Weekly*, Vol. 34, pp. 5190–204.

Malinowski, Bronislaw, 1922, *Argonauts of the Western Pacific: An Account of Native Enterprises and Adventure in the Archipelagoes of Melanesia, New Guinea* (London: Routledge and Kegan Paul).

Marshall, T.H., 1977, *Class, Citizenship and Social Development* (Chicago: University of Chicago Press).

Matsushita, Masaharu, 1996, *The Mind of Management* (Kadoma, Osaka: Matsushita Electrical and Industrial Company).

Mitford, Nancy, 1989, *Noblesse Oblige* (Oxford: Oxford University Press).

Parsons, Talcott, 1959, *The Structure of Social Action* (New Delhi: Amerind Press).

Power, M., 1994, *The Audit Explosion* (London: Demos).

Power, M., 1997, *The Audit Society: The Rituals of Verification* (Oxford: Oxford Univeristy Press).

Rawls, John, 1971, *A Theory of Justice* (Cambridge, Massachusetts: Belknaps Press, Harvard University).

Report of the Study Group on Women and Child Labour, 2001, (New Delhi: National Commission on Labour).

von Hayek, F. A., 1967, *Studies in Philosophy, Politics and Economics* (London: Routledge).

Young, Michael and Peter Willmott, 1973, *The Symmetrical Family: A Study of Work and Leisure in the London Region* (London: Routledge and Kegan Paul).

INDEX

ABOUT THE AUTHOR

Dipankar Gupta is Professor, Centre for the Study of Social Systems, Jawaharlal Nehru University, New Delhi. He has been a Visiting Professor at the University of Toronto, Institut D'Etudes Politiques in Paris and Lille, and at the University of Strasbourg. He was also a Fulbright Fellow in 1998, Visiting Fellow at Maison des Sciences de L'Homme, Paris, and Charles Wallace Fellow at the University of Hull. In 2003, he was the Leverhulme Visiting Professor at the London School of Economics. His research interests include modernization and citizenship, caste and stratification, and ethnicity and politics.

Professor Gupta is the co-editor of the journal, *Contributions to Indian Sociology*. His latest publications include *Mistaken Modernity: India Between Worlds* (2000), *Culture, Space and the Nation-State* (2000), *Interrogating Caste* (2000), and *Learning to Forget: The Anti-Memoirs of Modernity* (2005).